QUIET
DESPERATION

WAITING

All my life I have been planning and hoping and thinking and dreaming and loitering and waiting. All my life I have been getting ready to begin to do something worth the while. I have been waiting for the summer and waiting for the fall; I have been waiting for the winter and waiting for the spring; waiting for the night and waiting for the morning; waiting and dawdling and dreaming, until the day is almost spent and the twilight close at hand.

—Clarence Darrow

QUIET DESPERATION

Plain Talk on Life and Death

by BILL WEINER

LYLE STUART INC.   SECAUCUS, N. J.

Queries regarding rights and permissions
should be addressed to Lyle Stuart Inc.,
120 Enterprise Ave., Secaucus, N. J. 07094

Published by Lyle Stuart Inc. Published simultaneously
in Canada by General Publishing Co. Limited
Don Mills, Ontario

Manufactured in the United States of America

Library of Congress Cataloging in Publication Data
Main entry under title:
Quiet desperation.

1. Death—United States—Public opinion.   2. Public
opinion—United States.   3. Middle aged men—United
States—Attitudes.   4. Aged—United States—Attitudes.
5. Middle aged—United States—Interview.   6. Aged—
United States—Interviews.   I. Weiner, Bill.
HQ1073.5.U6Q53   155.9′37   80-36669
ISBN 0-8184-0303-9

*This book is dedicated to Paul McWilliams,
my friend and mentor*

Contents

Acknowledgments

It is not possible to express adequate thanks to all the people with whom I have spoken in the course of this work. In sharing a part of their lives with me, they have enriched my life immeasurably. It goes without saying that there would be no book without them. To those whose words appear in these pages and to the many more who, although not represented here, have also contributed much to this book, I am deeply grateful.

I also wish to thank those individuals in the nursing homes, rest homes, hospitals, and other institutions I visited who allowed me the opportunity to speak with the people there. I am grateful for their cooperation and kind assistance.

I am indebted to Studs Terkel, whose books *Division Street, Hard Times,* and *Working* provided the original impetus to begin this work; to David Futornick and the members of RAW for their support and encouragement; and to Traudi Weiner, Carole Livingston, Lyle Stuart, Allan Wilson, Marvin Rodin, and my parents for all that they have done.

I am especially grateful to Estelle Borker, Helen Howard, Gertrude Bondy, Lucille Carr, Heidi Hilzensauer, and Karen Weiner for believing in me when I didn't believe in myself.

Last, I want to thank Audrey Weiner, my lover, friend, and editor, who suffered along with me and sustained me through all the stages of this book. Without her love, support, enthusiasm, ideas, criticism, and hard work, this book would never have become a reality.

I am grateful to the following publishers, authors, and authors' representatives for permission to quote from the works named below:

BLACK SPARROW PRESS for an excerpt from "Some Brilliant Sky" by Diane Wakoski, from *Dancing on the Grave of a Son of a Bitch.* Copyright © 1973 by Diane Wakoski. Reprinted by permission of Black Sparrow Press.

DODD, MEAD AND COMPANY, INC. for "The Sceptic" by Robert Service, from *The Collected Poems of Robert Service.* Copyright 1912 by

QUIET
DESPERATION

The rocks at which he clutched were worn smooth and slippery by time and the water. He clung to each as he came to it. The relentless water tore him loose every time, and pushed him on as effortlessly as if he were a leaf or an insect on the surface. He was helpless, out of control, beyond the power of human effort. As coldly as the water sucking at his ankles, as surely as it pounded him from the deceptive rocks, Wicker knew there was nothing he could do. That was the moment in which he had recognized, not his life played back before his eyes, but the iron indifference of things, the blind chance by which the world in its turning and life in its passing struck down men and objects alike, and went on unchanged. In that moment of awful vision into the heart of the matter, Wicker had not been afraid, precisely because there was nothing he could do, no way he could fail, crack, escape, make things worse or better for himself or anyone. For once, he need not even try to be worthy, for no one could be worthy of a force so powerful and so uncaring and so flawlessly impartial that it merely swept before it what was there. . . .

Later—a long time later, it had seemed—the same impersonal force that had taken him down threw him up again and as carelessly, far downstream, against a ledge where he could grasp dry rock above the water. He had never known how he came to be the only man ever to plunge over the Great Falls and live; but that chance could be no different from—in fact, was a part of—the chance that could have killed him, in an indifference so perfect that it made no distinction between life and death.

—Tom Wicker

Introduction

In a sense, this book has had a life of its own. I began four years ago talking with older people about their life experiences. I visited a few local nursing homes and rest homes and began speaking with the residents there. It was more or less an experiment. I had no idea what direction the book would take or for that matter if there would be a book at all.

Over the next few months, I spoke with forty or fifty people. The subject of death came up quite often in our conversations, although it was not something I initiated; in fact, in the beginning I would attempt to direct the conversation to something more "pleasant." Since I was uncomfortable with the subject, in my naïveté I assumed they were also. In time, my curiosity got the best of me; I stopped changing the subject and began asking questions.

As I became aware of how important it was for people to have someone to talk to and express their feelings about death, I found myself becoming increasingly interested in how we view our lives in relation to our own mortality. In hopes of discovering some of the ways our lives are shaped by this vision and are affected by the experience of death, I decided to take the book in that direction, broadening its scope to include people of all ages and backgrounds.

In the course of sixteen months, I spoke with close to four hundred people, forty-four of whom are represented in these pages. All of the conversations were informal, no prepared questions were used. The conversations, some very brief, others taking place over a few days or several weeks, were tape-recorded. The tapes were later transcribed and then edited. Everything you will read is in the person's own words, presented in the form of stories, poems or prose poems. The greatest difficulty I encountered while working on this book was in translating the spoken word into the written word. Too often, so much is lost in this process. I was not able to include many of the people to whom I had spoken, having to limit myself to those whose words I felt I could do justice.

Death ultimately touches each one of us. Although it is an experience we all have in common, it influences each of us differently. Through an understanding of the various ways in which death affects our lives, perhaps we can come to a better understanding of ourselves. I hope this book will contribute to that understanding.

*   *   *

With some exceptions, in order to insure confidentiality the names used throughout are pseudonyms. An asterisk appearing after a name denotes that the person's real name has been used.

1
Perspectives

LIFE AND DEATH

The two old, simple problems ever intertwined,
Close home, elusive, present, baffled, grappled.
By each successive age insoluble, pass'd on,
To ours to-day—and we pass on the same.
                                        —Walt Whitman

The Job

Paul Lander, forty-eight, has been a homicide detective for the past fifteen years.

Death is death. That's all there's to it. It's something we deal with every day. You never get emotional. There's no personal feelings. My dog got killed by a car, I cried like a baby; but somebody else . . . it's just a job.

The guys I work with have a very strange, almost sadistic sense of humor. I mean, if somebody coughs, they say he's got cancer. This girl shot herself. We found her all crumpled up on the bathroom floor. The jokes come out: "That's a helluva good looking broad; man, the undertaker's gonna have a ball tonight." It's sick, but you're doing a sick job.

We see all kinds of death. You don't think in terms of people—it's causes: homicide, suicide, accidental, coronary, and so on. You got a guy down in the morgue, you go down and see what happened to him. So the guy's dead. That body's just a piece of meat; just something you work with to find out the cause. It's a job.

There Is Something to Figure Out
About Being Alive

Jane Brandmeir, twenty-five, is a visiting nurse. For the past month, she has been working with a woman dying of cancer.

> *Good Lord, I don't know what "rights" a man has!*
> *And I don't know the solution of boredom. If I did,*
> *I'd be the one philosopher that had the cure for*
> *living. But I do know that about ten times as many*
> *people find their lives dull, and unnecessarily dull,*
> *as ever admit it; and I do believe that if we busted*
> *out and admitted it sometimes, instead of being*
> *nice and patient and loyal for sixty years, and then*
> *nice and patient and dead for the rest of eternity,*
> *why, maybe, possibly, we might make life more*
> *fun.*
> —Sinclair Lewis

There are so many things I don't understand. There is something to figure out about being alive, and I certainly need to do it. Working with people who are crippled and people who are dying has made me more conscious of my life. It's like . . . okay, here I am at twenty-five, what am I going to do to fill the space between now and whenever death comes. You know, just what are the things that are important for me to do, and what are the things that are important for me not to do.

Understanding that death happens makes you realize more what you want to do and gives you the incentive to act on it. It made me realize that, fuck it, I'm not gonna

16

live my life by what other people say. I mean, I've got to be a "good" girl, be married, have kids, and be faithful and stuff like that.

It made me more aware of my own strength and how I want to live my life. I have the potential to be very happy, very fruitful, very alive. I'm not cancerous. I'm aware of the life that I have in me and what I'm going to do with it to make it special, so when I get around to dying, I'll be satisfied with myself.

Rigor Mortis

George Osborne, fifty-six, is the son of a funeral director and has followed his father's profession all of his adult life.

I see so much death that I've gotten to the point where I have accepted the idea that death is a part of life. If I'm told that somebody died who I had just seen a half-hour ago, it doesn't upset me. It might, if it was my own family, but friends that I have known for years . . . that doesn't upset me. If I'm told that somebody had died suddenly . . . so he died. I feel sorry for the family, but it's not as upsetting to me as it is for some people.

I've reached a point—you might call it hardness or callousness. When Mother and Dad passed away, I was there and I did some of the work just to see it was done the way I wanted it to be done. It didn't bother me at all. It's not that I wasn't emotionally upset when I lost both Mother and Dad —I worked with Dad side by side all these years, and that's a little bit closer than a lot of people get to their father; and of course I saw Mother every day, she lived upstairs—but death to me is part of life, and you must face it. It's gonna happen to all of us, and if it happens . . . that's the way it goes.

O Death, Where Is Thy Sting?

Sidney Rosen, forty-two, is part-owner of a large suburban memorial park.

When people find out what business I'm in, they'll say, "Sidney, you're in a business that people are just dying to get in." I tell 'em, "Yeah, that's the one thousand, three hundred and thirty-second time I've heard that one, but I appreciate you bringing it up anyway, I always get a kick out of it."

I find that people tend to seek me out, or give me a little more attention, or they are a little more friendly than they would normally be to me as a person. I can't put my finger

19

on it, but I think there is something about the kind of work that I do that intrigues them. People ask me how I can work here—isn't it morbid working in a cemetery? I kid 'em and tell them, "No, when we get 'em, they're gift wrapped."

When the postman brings in a small container of cremated remains, I usually kid him and say, "You got another instant person. Just add water. . . ."

I think most people in the cemetery business do it as anyone would do any other job, whether it's tasteful or distasteful, whether he be a doctor or a garbage collector. I don't think a garbage collector worries about garbage on his off hours . . . neither do I worry about death.

Studying Death

Ann O'Donnell, fifty-two, had been a registered nurse for more than twenty years. She left nursing to pursue a career in psychology and is currently teaching and working towards a doctorate.

> *Men fear death, as children fear to go in the dark;*
> *and as that natural fear in children is increased*
> *with tales, so is the other.*
>   —Francis Bacon

I became interested in teaching about death because of a close call I had with death myself. After I had recovered, the doctor said to me, "Do you know how close to death you were?" I began thinking. I didn't know and I wondered how many other people have been so close to the end and haven't realized it. I thought back to the time when I was an R.N., and about all the cancer patients I saw who knew they were going to die and yet nobody would say, "Yes, you're gonna die." I thought about all the lies I told patients and the games we played concerning death.

There is this tremendous anxiety syndrome that's built up around this fear of death and dying. Doctors deal with death and dying; it's part of their workday. The opportunity for them to talk about it is certainly greater than some guy who sells cars, but they don't want to talk about death. It's a taboo-like veil that they've thrown over the subject—kind of shove it under the rug like so much dust.

In just the same way that the gynecologist or the obstetrician cannot talk to his patient about sexual matters because he is uncomforable with it, I would say that there are just as many physicians who can't talk about death because they're uncomfortable. I can remember a surgeon who would operate on a patient, open the patient, see that it was cancer, close the patient up and go to pieces. He would literally say, "Goddamn son of a bitch; look at this, here's another cancer, it's metastatic; we're not gonna be able to help this person." From that point on that physician could not go to that patient other than to say good morning. By the same token, if he could cure the patient, it's a different ball game entirely.

We've got to do something about the fact that we don't level with patients. Many of these doctors are so detached from the humanistic aspects of medicine. They're bent on preservation of life at all costs; save a life, save a life. They're clinicians, they're operators, they're mechanics and that's it. So many of these doctors will say, "I'm not a shrink; if you got a problem coping, adjusting, whatever, you better go see a psychiatrist, that's what they're for. I deal with your chest, not your head." To me that's incongruous. You've got to treat the whole person.

I knew all of these things and thought that we ought to do something about this whole topic of death and dying. Soon after I recovered, I went back to college. I had to look for a dissertation topic. I wrote up a proposal dealing with death and the value of death education. I did a hell of a lot of research, and the more books I read, the more I became fascinated with it.

For some reason or other, my dissertation advisor decided that it might not be an appropriate topic for me to research. It was kind of like ten years ago when we were doing this exposition of human sexuality and were wondering just how much we could get into the curriculum of the schools. I had no idea that people would reject a curriculum on death in much the same way that they did on human sexuality.

Parents are still not too sure whether or not they think

school personnel should be the ones to tell their kids about death. I don't think that you can suddenly begin to discuss this when a person is post-adolescent. Like human sexuality, I think we have to begin at the beginning. The way to do that is to discuss the way in which a child thinks about death. When children are very young they fantasize. When they get a little older they begin to see cause-and-effect relationships between what they do, and how it might cause death. Mother says, "Don't go out into the street because something might happen to you." Well, what might happen? I might get killed. If very early in life one begins to talk about death and dying—the flower died, the plant died, the dog died, my grandfather died—finally one day the child can say, "*I'm* gonna die." The connection between the biological self and death can be seen.

We usually get anxious about things we don't know about. Since there is no opportunity for empirical research, since we cannot appeal to others who have died, the best we can do is simulate, talk about what it is like to die, and what does it mean. Death education is important; not because you learn so much, but because you're able to open your mind to different ways of thinking about death. When you think about it, you talk about it; and when you talk about it, you become more comfortable with it.

We can liken it to people who don't like to look at pornography, or people who don't like to swear. For some people to say the word penis or vagina, or screwing, or even sexual intercourse, is difficult. I once attended a seminar on human sexuality where they made people say words like fuck. The first time a person said fuck, he might think, why should I have to use this expression? Then everyone sat around in a group and kind of fiddled around with expressions like, that fucking so and so, that fucking jerk, or whatever. Once you got over the initial shock, you could use the words and hear them without cringing in your seat.

You became familiar with them, and because of that you

weren't so shocked. If I'm out in a public place and some-body walks in and says, "This fucking place stinks," I would probably say to myself, that's not necessary at all. By the same token, if I read the word fuck in literature, I don't say, oh my God, I'm gonna put this damn thing down, I'm not gonna read it, because I think that it is a way to express things. That's what I mean with familiarity; not so much that I'm going to run around saying, "Oh, it's a fucking nice day out."

DIE, DIE, DEATH, DEATH. Once you can use these words and hear these words and get over the initial shock, you can begin to talk about death and dying in a sensible way. To understand that everybody has to die is important. Ultimately, you are going to die, and the more you say it to yourself, the more accustomed you become to it. When you hear that somebody has died, you don't have to say that he passed on, he passed away, he went to heaven, or any of the other euphemisms. You know he's dead, but by saying "He passed away," you can deny or avoid the death for a while.

Avoidance is not a healthy way to cope. Now if you can say *he died,* and let it go at that, and realize, I'll never see him again, I'll never laugh with him again, I'll never cry with him again, the concept of the lack of physical presence becomes familiar, and you can accept it and adjust to the finality.

Whatever we can do to provide learning experiences about death and to decrease anxiety and fear is important. There is no panacea. The best that we can do is to stimulate discussions, to put people in situations where they can have their minds opened and think.

*　　*　　*

I don't think of any thought processes beyond, into the supernatural or any of that. They're gonna put me in the ground or they're gonna cremate me and that would be the end. I'm not irreligious, not without some religious thought, but I don't know that there is anything beyond this particular life. In ten years I might change. As I get older and closer to death, I might suddenly, you know, get that "old time religion."

I'm not ready to die. I have a lot that I still want to do; I have a lot of energy that I want to use up. I guess what I want is to memorialize myself in as many different ways as I possibly can. I have two children, and that in itself is memorialization. What I'm waiting for now is grandchildren. I wish to memorialize myself professionally; I want to be a good enough teacher to have left an impact on lots of people.

I believe in longevity. If I'm supposed to live to be seventy-eight, yeah, let me live to seventy-eight. If I can go five years beyond that, it's icing on the cake. That's all I ask.

The Administrator

Pamela Lyons, thirty-six, is the administrator of a private nursing home.

Her mind lives in a quiet room,
A narrow room, and tall,
With pretty lamps to quench the gloom
And mottoes on the wall.

There all the things are waxen neat
And set in decorous lines;
And there are posies, round and sweet,
And little, straightened vines.

Her mind lives tidily, apart
From cold and noise and pain,
And bolts the door against her heart,
Out wailing in the rain.
                                    —Dorothy Parker

I would say we have . . . oh, at least one death a week . . . maybe more. Over the weekend we had five expire—it just worked out that way. As soon as it's noted that a patient has expired, the doctor is called immediately and the family is notified. The doctor must come in to pronounce the body dead. That's our state law, the body can't be moved until that time. The curtain is pulled until the funeral parlor comes in for the body. The effects are placed in a suitcase or plastic bag.

The body is usually taken out through the rear entrance

26

—*not* the front entrance. The funeral parlors have instructions to use the delivery back entrance so that the other patients here are not . . . you know, confronted with that. We don't cordon off the building and have everybody not come out of their rooms because a body is removed through the hallway, but the body is . . . you know, covered.

The grapevine here is very quick and usually the patients are aware that somebody has expired. Nobody really says anything. I have never, in the time I have been here, ever heard one patient refer, you know, to another patient's death. It's just not mentioned. It is accepted very much so as far as I have observed . . . of course, I don't know what their conversation is amongst themselves when I am not here.

If you become friendly or involved with many people here, you know, within a few months or weeks or whatever, they are no longer here. I do not become emotionally involved, because if I did I could not function as effectively. Possibly because I have the attitude that I do, I can continue working here as objectively as I do.

I have had conversations with individual patients who had requested death. In other words, they want to die. Usually these patients are the hardest to involve in anything. Whatever the circumstances for their being here, for some reason they feel rejected by their family; they feel the family doesn't want them, and that's why they were put here, and they just might as well die. This is what their family wants—all right, they are going to make it come true.

I get the daily reports from the nurses and it might say: Mrs. So-and-So, very depressed today; refused to eat; refused medication . . . whatever. It's the same old story, especially with a new admission. I usually make it my business that I see the patient every day for just a cheerful "hi" and "isn't it a nice day today."

*   *   *

My attitude towards death is that it is a part of life—it's something that happens. My feeling towards death is that, especially for the elderly, it's okay. If you made it to seventy, seventy-five, eighty, I think you are pretty lucky and whatever you have done prior to, you know, coming to a nursing home and dying, you have had control up to that point and you either made it or you didn't make it. When they come here and their lives are governed by nurses and medication, to me, personally, they are no longer living, really. It's over. Because life to me is activity.

I very rarely think about death related to myself—why bother, I'm here. I don't even plan for the future; I don't like to do that. I very rarely plan a vacation in advance because I don't want to be disappointed if something doesn't work out. That's the way I like to live. I don't plan, so therefore I'm not disappointed.

I don't like to think about death; the finality, what's it all mean, why are we put here, what's it all about . . . was it all worth it. I don't think about coming to grips with the fact that, hey, I'm not going to be here some day. Maybe it's because I'm afraid, but I don't like to think about those things. I know I'm not going to be here one day. It doesn't affect my life-style. I just get up every day and do what I like to do. That's generally how I live life, and if I die tomorrow, okay.

I don't brood about it; it doesn't upset me. I think I would like not to die. If I could live forever actively, fine . . . but I don't know if I would like to do that either because there would be . . . you know, so many more disappointments and suffering, and maybe there is a point when a person doesn't want to experience pain, suffering, and disappointments anymore.

Ministering to the Dying

Charles Hummel, forty-one, is a Protestant hospital chaplain.

When I was about nine or ten, I had a very good friend who lived down the street from me. He was a particularly nice kid and well liked. I recall I had a childhood infatuation with his sister. He contracted polio; in those days polio was extremely serious and there was a high mortality rate. He died, and I remember going to his viewing. It was in his house, and I remember seeing him in the coffin with flowers all around.

I guess I must have been pretty frightened. I can't get in touch with any feelings, probably because I wasn't allowed to at the time. I don't recall talking to my parents about it and expressing any feelings. I do remember just being in my room that night, which indicates to me that it was a solitary experience. I also remember the next day in school telling my teacher about it. The teacher's response was very flip: "Well, that's too bad, but it's something we all have to go through."

I think this was typical of the kind of experience children have with death. They are not credited with the ability to cope with this and are shut out. I think it's the height of insensitivity to disallow children these feelings because it is going to come back and haunt them. It's going to be part of their whole feeling system. When children are not involved in a crisis like this and have no reality to relate to, more often than not the vacuum is filled with a sense of dread, fear, and mystery.

I am convinced that it manifested itself during my teen years. I had a horrendous fear of death; a fear so pervasive that it robbed me of the ability to live. One of the greatest terrors I had was of flunking out of school. To me that meant death. Death doesn't have to be thought of as *dead* dead; death can also manifest itself in a fear of risk-taking or in terms of becoming involved with other people. It shows itself in many very destructive ways. In my case I think it was played out in terms of my relationships with other people, my feelings of inadequacy, and my tremendous fear of failure, which is directly related to the fear of death —the ultimate failure.

I somehow picked up this Germanic idea that illness was an affront. To be sick was *Verboten*. It was a sign of weakness. You weren't supposed to get sick, and if you got sick, *Ach du Lieber!* Even if it was just a bloomin' cold, there was something vaguely bad about it, and in a sense you were punished for it. This wasn't blatant, but it was implied in the treatment. I was confined to my room—not because I was a bad boy, but implicit in this sort of thing was that you're a threat: Don't give me your cold. So there was this implied punitive measure, you were put in solitary; you were put in bed—for a kid that's punishment. You got to feeling, Oh, God, what did I do?

*   *   *

In the hospital, guilt is always associated with illness. It may be an unconscious kind of thing, but there is a sub-liminal floating feeling of guilt. It may be in the guise of religious language: "Why did God do this to me," or it just may be, "I did something wrong," or "I am a burden on my family." When illness involves hospitalization, there is always regression. We regress back to a semi-childlike status. We become dependent. It's like reintroducing the umbili-cal cord. In terms of symbolism, it's very visible, you've got the I.V.'s. All of this can conspire to make a person feel less than what he or she is. It runs counter to a person's self-image. You feel worthless; you're a burden.

Take a man, an executive. He has a coronary. You take him away from his work and put him in a hospital where he cannot push a button and tell his secretary what to do, or pick up a phone and bark orders at his colleagues. His routine is dictated to him on someone else's terms. You've got a real basket case on your hands. I'm exaggerating a little bit, but the point I'm trying to make is that illness is an affront. It induces a sense of non-productivity and worthlessness, and this is a cancerous kind of thing. It can take on dimensions all out of proportion. A person's sense of worth can be so intimidated and the feelings generated by that may, and often do, begin to include his whole life.

We need to be aware of this. A person's self-image, his capacity to feel and his coping mechanisms are very closely tied together. We need to pay attention to a person's feeling of worth. I find that my main function is to engage a patient in conversation, in a dialogue about him or herself. I try to zoom in on those positive aspects and to draw them out; to remind a patient of things which may have been repressed.

The way people cope with death is going to follow a pattern of how they cope with life. My mother had a very real problem with self-image all her life. She was a very effective person; she carried out her affairs beautifully. She was a constructive, organized and productive person, and yet she had a gnawing sense of inferiority. When she became ill with cancer, it became a very real problem. In our conversations together during her last year, I felt that my responsibility to her and myself was to reinforce the fact that she was a good, moral person and that her life had worth.

In terms of helping a person die with dignity, this is crucial. A person who has a terminal illness has a real need to be able to look back on his or her life and say that it

was a good one. I think the most poignant, difficult cases
are those people who think that they have never amounted
to anything and have relegated their lives to the garbage
can.

We live in an achievement-oriented society. It is ingrained in us that you are supposed to be a productive
member of society. Our sense of worth is premised on how
much we produce. I think one of the symptoms of the
pathology in our culture is that we tend to equate a person's
worth with his or her achievements.

An horrendous example of this occurred several years
ago. A driver, under the influence of barbiturates, ran off
the road and struck three children. Two were killed instantly and the other child was thrown clear and survived.
The father of two of the children is a very close friend of
mine, and I sat in on some of the court proceedings. The
monetary settlement was premised on the fact that the children were non-productive citizens. In other words, if they
had been adults and had been "productive citizens," their
monetary value would have increased proportionately; but,
because they were children, the settlement was significantly
less. It's absolutely incredible, but I think this points up our
whole orientation. If you produce, you are worth something
and the criterion of worth is really dollars and cents.

*   *   *

I think the most difficult time I have, the most difficult
conditions I can imagine, is when there is a conspiracy of
silence. The husband may ask me to go see his wife but not
to talk to her about dying. "We know she is dying, but we
don't want to upset her." For me to get involved and add
to that situation is horrendous. I'm a very lousy actor and
I just can't bluff. It's awful; you are playing a game, putting
up a façade, and you're as phoney as a three-dollar bill.

The situation in which I feel okay—which doesn't mean

comfortable, is where I feel the freedom to express emotions: to express fear in the presence of a patient, to get
angry, to cry or to laugh; whatever. To get involved, to talk
about a person's life and encourage the person to talk about
his or her feelings, or just sit there and hold hands; then
I feel like a human being.

My first experience of being present with a patient and
his family at the time of death was perhaps one of the most
exhilarating experiences one can imagine. I was really quite
surprised. It had a lot to do with my relationship with the
person, with the nature of his dying process, and his relationship to his family. It was really a very beautiful experience.
It was almost an ideal situation in that all opportunities
were present for dealing with death in an open, honest way.
The patient preparing himself and preparing us, and the
actual experience of the moment of death, was a deeply
religious one. It was fraught with great spiritual significance
and had absolutely no relationship with fear or morbidity.
There was a deep sense of intimacy amongst us, and the
overall feeling was one of great peace.

*　　　*　　　*

We have been trained and conditioned to think that to
be young, robust, and productive is the ideal, but aging is
an affront. I am constantly at war with what I have been
taught about aging: it's bad, it's sad, it's threatening. The
anxiety is always there. I am very much aware of my fears
of the debilitating and restricting effects of aging.

People seem to be dying younger. I don't know the
statistics, but it seems that way to me. Right now I'm working with about three or four cancer patients. There is one
in his late forties and another in her late fifties. I consider
that young—at least I hope that's young. I'm very much
aware of the approach of middle age. I'm forty now—I say
I'm forty but I'm actually forty-one. I have a hard time

getting past that forty. I think probably until I'm forty-five or forty-six, I'm going to say I'm forty. Maybe never. That's a hang-up with me.

When you are dealing with your contemporaries, you are up against the possibility that it could be you. It's possible for me to get cancer; it's possible for me to have a coronary. I know Mr. Smith, Mr. Jones and Mrs. Gottrocks have had heart attacks, and they're forty-one, forty-four and forty-eight. It's sobering, but you still deny it. I hear myself saying, Gee, I'm thin, I get lots of exercise, I eat okay, I sleep okay, I'm not under stress. Part of me says, No, I'm not going to get a heart attack, but the other part says, You know, it's a possibility. I just don't know. I really can't talk about my fear of death because I can't conceive of it.

*   *   *

I've become much more aware of the intensity of my need to get the hell out at the end of the day and put distance between me and here. It's a form of denial, but it's a necessary thing. I've just got to get away. I've got to transport myself from that which suggests limitations, incapacity, and threats to my being, to that which enhances it. I've become aware of what I have to do for me, whether it's going for a swim or a bike ride, working in my garden or walking in the woods, or listening to music. All of these things simply trigger a counter-reminder that I have my legs, my mobility, and that I have an emotional capacity for enjoyment.

One of the things I have become increasingly aware of is that I'm thinking less and less about the future and more and more about today, tomorrow and maybe a couple of days from now. I've become a lot more extravagant in terms of spending my money and indulging myself. I find myself really much more aware of the need to fulfill my immediate life with everything I possibly can.

I find it necessary to engage in things which get me out of myself a little bit and put me in touch with the physical universe. I was talking about this with one of my colleagues —he's about the same age as myself and also a chaplain. He said that he had developed an interest in astronomy which he never had before. He finds tremendous release and satisfaction in literally throwing himself in the sky. This is his way of coping. He identifies with the agelessness of the universe, which is another way of expressing one's hope for eternal life.

I have found my own concept of eternal life changing radically in the last couple of years. When I look at a sunset, or when I am walking in the woods; when I look at a flower, when I hear the wind, or I am out on the ocean, my growing conviction is that in some way I'm going to be part of that.

I believe that there is a transcendent consciousness. I feel very deeply that this consciousness is a part of the created order. I have watched people actually die. I just cannot come away from that experience without a very deep, gut feeling that something very significant happens to the psyche as the body goes from life to death. When the psyche, spirit, soul, whatever you want to call it, goes through that transition, the expression on a person's face gives itself over to complete relaxation and there is a tremendous aura of peace. I don't want to sound romantic or fanciful, but it is difficult for me to watch this and not come away with a sense of awe and a profound conviction that whatever lies on the other side is basically, fundamentally benevolent, and that this transition is not something to stand in terror of.

*   *   *

My earliest childhood experience with death was when my dog was hit by a car. I went out of the house and left the door open and the little fellow ran out into the street. The relationship between children and animals is an important one. There is a commonality there. I think children instinctively identify with animals. I suppose some analysts would see some very primitive things going on here in terms of our collective unconscious, our relationship with the animal world and the animal that is within us. Not so much the animal per se, but the instinctive, primitive, elemental drives that we really share in common with the animal. We do try to set ourselves apart, and I think that a great deal of our ecological problems that we are having today have their origins there. I think the more we forget, the more that we try to repress the fact that we are part of a created order and we are animalistic in many ways, the more dangerous we become.

I think that people who are closest to the earth, whose roots are in the earth, whose life support system is the earth, have a profound respect for their milieu, for their environment. They don't tamper with it and they treat it with genuine respect. These people, I have discovered, have the healthiest response to death.

This became very clear to me in the five years I spent with farmers out in Pennsylvania. Not only do these people live among and witness the life and death process of animals, but they live close to the earth; and in terms of the change of seasons, the earth has its own symbolic death and resurrection. That is not to say that death was not a source of mourning and sorrow, but there was not this terror, this hostility, this outrage towards death as if it is something that is perpetrated upon us and ought not to be. Death was a felt phenomenon in its relationship to the whole scheme of things.

In our more urban areas, where we have gotten further away from our elemental commonness with our evironment, with our natural habitat, the more alienated we become from natural phenomena such as death. It then becomes a source of fear and deep-seated resentment, and this is unhealthy. The further we get away from our own naturalness and the more artificial we become, I think the more difficult life and death become.

2

The Threat of Death

Life and death are the only issues;
we often forget that—
arranging our furniture,
washing our cars.

—Diane Wakoski

Outwitting Death

Michael Willner,* thirty-two, is a practicing attorney.

I was suffering from what I felt was some sort of bad indigestion. I went to the doctor, and he did some preliminary blood work and ran some tests. Initially he thought I had hepatitis, but shortly after decided that the blood he took was not fully indicative of hepatitis. They did a couple of biopsies and weren't satisfied. Finally, they decided to do open surgery to look at my liver and to take some samples from different parts of my body to look at under a microscope. At that time the doctor told me that I had to consider the possibility that I had cancer of the liver, but because of my age it was remote.

They put me into a room with a fellow who was dying of stomach cancer; he was about thirty years old and I understand he has since died. That was a little bit scary, and it didn't do a tremendous amount of good for my morale; although I suppose I rationalized it because I said to myself, Well, if the chances are that young people don't get it and he has it and his number is up, maybe my number isn't.

I tried to look on the bright side and be optimistic about it. I didn't treat it as a joke, although the night before the operation I remember I got into the medicine cabinet on

the hall and with Merthiolate wrote the word THINK
across my stomach. I wanted to write DO NOT OPEN
UNTIL CHRISTMAS, but there wasn't enough room. The
surgeon didn't see it until after I was asleep, but he reported
to me later that I was a real comedian, and if he had
laughed any harder he would have cut something off.

It turned out I didn't have cancer, which I was delighted
to hear—but that's the good news. The bad news is that I
had something called scleroscing cholangitis with biliary
cirrhosis.

*   *   *

In the beginning, he beat around the bush a little bit and
I said, "Look, just tell me if I'm going to live, and if I'm
not going to live, how long do I have." I didn't want anybody to tell me half-truths or break it to me gently. I wanted
to hear it and get it over with. I heard it. He said, "Okay, I
think you may live to forty but probably not much longer
than that."

It was shocking, but when somebody tells you that you are
going to die or there is some chance you are going to die, I
suppose the initial reaction is to discard it altogether; but
after that you have to think . . . well, maybe . . . you know,
maybe I am, and if I am, what am I going to do. I had to
make some plans with my life. At that time I had a little girl
almost two and I was very concerned about leaving her without a father.

I remember driving home and thinking about it, but I
didn't decide to drive my car off the George Washington
Bridge on account of it. I think committing suicide is the
ultimate cop-out, the ultimate quit, and I just . . . it's a
matter of pride. I don't think I would want people to walk
around saying, "Oh, Mike Willner, he couldn't make it, he
couldn't cut it, he checked out." No matter how bad things

got, I would want to be able to look back later and say things were awful and I prevailed; I remained in control of my circumstances and myself, and I won. Fate did not win. I won.

I think between the time the doctor told me and the time I got home I decided I was not going to talk to anybody about it. I didn't tell my wife or my parents. It wasn't that I refused to believe it, but I was going to fight it as long as I could. I am of the belief that survival has a lot to do with your outlook and your desire to live.

You can call it strength or you can call it weakness. It may take strength to be able to hold it in; but on the other hand, it takes strength to fess up and tell people things that you know are going to cause a lot of unpleasantness to both them and you.

I didn't think it would do any good at all. In fact, I think it would have been bad; I didn't want to frighten people. If you are dying, the doctors are doing the best they can to help you; there is nothing anybody else can do. Why make them miserable. I am selfish. I don't want to make them miserable, because it would make me miserable to be around them. I just couldn't stand to be around gloomy people; maybe I didn't have the strength to put up with a bunch of glooms, so it was out of weakness that I refrained from telling them.

I don't think I would want to use it as a weapon or a sympathy device; I think that would really be dirty pool. I can remember when I was a little boy and on occasion being punished and sent to my room. I went there crying, and I remember fantasizing in my mind, boy, wouldn't they be sorry if I was dead; then they would realize how much they should have appreciated me. But the problem was that I wouldn't have been around to enjoy seeing it. I think that our character makeup is partially what we are born with and partially what we acquire through our environment. I guess that's the way I am. I don't think it's anything to be praised or lauded or looked down upon. It's just . . . that's me. If you want to be completely fatalistic about the whole thing, maybe it was predictable that I would react that way and it really didn't take anything special on my part. I was more or less programmed to act that way. It was just a reaction; my normal reaction. If somebody stepped on my toe, I would say ouch; when somebody told me that I was going to die, I think this was my normal reaction.

*   *   *

Without trying to pat myself on the back too hard, I think that I have led a very moral life. That doesn't mean that I didn't go out and commit "sins." I think I'm very idealistic about telling the truth and about integrity and honesty and things like that. I've been brought up to believe that's the right way to live, and I have lived that way. It would be hard for me to be a liar; I don't think I would be a very good liar. It would be hard for me to be a crook. I don't feel that there is anything that I should have done differently. I feel I have met most of the standards that I have set up for myself.

I think the things I want are pretty ordinary. I would like to have a nice standard of living and be able to educate my children and make sure that they have everything they need and a lot of things that they want. I don't think that I became frustrated over not being able to accomplish . . . having climbed Mount Everest, or making a million dollars or something. I'm not consumed by any desire to own a home at the shore, a home in the mountains, a home in Florida, and drive Lincoln Continentals and Cadillacs. I don't need any monuments. I don't expect anybody to build a statue of me. I don't expect there to be a Michael Willner Memorial Law Library anywhere or a university law school named after me.

I don't expect to go to heaven or hell. I think when you die you're dead. It's one of the facts of life—it's the punch line. I just want those people who love me to remember me well. I think if I am remembered in a good way by people who are close to me—I think if my children have good memories of me, the way I can remember my two grandfathers—I guess that's the kind of immortality that I want.

I did make arrangements to have my eyes left to the Eye Bank and the rest of my body to the New Jersey College of Medicine and Dentistry. Whatever's left, I don't really care what they do with it; they can bury it or they can cremate me.

The other day I had a husband and wife in here who wanted a will drawn. They were very religious members of the Baptist faith. I think that they probably believed that people who are not Baptists are damned. The husband expressed a desire that he wanted to be cremated, and his wife was a little bit horrified by that. She wanted him to be buried in a cemetery with a nice tombstone. The more she insisted that he shouldn't be cremated, the more he insisted that he wanted to be. Finally, he instructed me to write a provision in his will to the effect that if he was not cremated, his entire estate would go to the Roman Catholic Church. At that point she capitulated and agreed to let him be cremated.

*   *   *

I think I enjoy living a lot more. It made me very appreciative of what I have. I do have a good family, a wonderful wife, and now I have two kids and another on the way. I also have a lot of very nice friends. I think it made

me enjoy being with them a lot more. I don't think it
changed the way I reacted towards them. I don't think I
developed any new interests but I think it renewed and
strengthened the interest I have in my family, and especially
my children. I play with them every night.

I try to leave my office at five-thirty and I go home and
I have dinner with my wife and kids. I give the kids a bath
and I usually dress the little boy for bed and I read to the
little girl. I work a lot of nights, but I do those things before I go out. I think it's important that they do know me,
and I'm sure in the back of my mind there is the thought
that if I die, at least they will know who I was and will
remember me.

I think that I have become impatient with people who
complain a lot. I suppose I've become a little bit intolerant
because I went through something that I had business to
complain about, and I didn't. Some people are always complaining. If you say, "How are you?" they say, "I can't
complain, it wouldn't do any good," and then they complain. I don't like to hear that. Complaining about things
that can't be helped to me is a big waste of time; all it does
is make the complainer and the complainee very unhappy.
In any event, I don't like to hear people crying the blues
and feeling sorry for themselves. They talk about the guy
who didn't have any shoes and he felt sorry for himself,
until he ran across somebody who didn't have any feet. I
think there is a lot of wisdom in that.

Sometimes you read about people who hear they have
a year to live, and they go out and they do all kinds of
bizarre things. They travel and try to accumulate as many
experiences as they can. Maybe if I had been told that I
have a year to live, I might have done the same thing. But
ten years is such a long time that death seems very remote.
Ten years ago I was twenty-two, and it's like another life
ago. The age of forty is almost another ten years off, and I

guess accepting that kind of death is different from the acceptance of a death within the next several months. We are all dying; we all know we are going to die some day.

I didn't constantly go around thinking that I am going to make the most of today because tomorrow I may not be here. I guess every time I heard that somebody died or was dying, it would make me think of myself; but I didn't go out and read treatises on the process of dying. Some people do, I guess, but ten years is almost as remote as living to full term, except that you know if you are going to die by the time you are forty, your kids are not going to be grown up when you die. That influenced and affected me, but it didn't make me change my lifestyle. You still have to pay the mortgage every month; you still have to pay the electric bill; and you still have to give your wife money to buy food every week; and for those things you have to go to work every day.

I don't think at any time I became morbid over it. I don't think I became bitter or jealous. I just know every morning when I woke up, I looked in the mirror and I would say to myself, Well, you're still here today."

*   *   *

I went on for about a year, every day waking up and thinking, Well, I'm alive again today. I never really felt bad, except I didn't like the way I looked; I was jaundiced and I looked funny. The doctors decided to try a medication called Prednisone, telling me probably it wouldn't work but they had to try something. Lo and behold, it worked. It didn't cure me; I still have the condition. But it changed the prognosis and brought everything under control. After two or three months of taking Prednisone, I was informed that I no longer had to fear dying around the age of forty, and that in good likelihood I would probably live to a normal age . . . although nobody made any promises.

I didn't turn cartwheels; I didn't go out and decide to get drunk and paint the town. I don't think I learned any great secrets. I didn't go to a guru. I didn't have any great religious inclination. I didn't get any pearls of wisdom from a rabbi or any other religious leader.

I think I was relieved. I felt reprieved—almost like somebody who has been given the death penalty being told that he has received a pardon from the governor. I was pleased; it was a very nice feeling, but it didn't change the way I live. It didn't change my lifestyle to find out that I was going to die, and it didn't change it to find out that I wasn't. I still appreciate my children, and I think that the good things that resulted from this situation have continued. Sometimes when you lose something or almost lose it, no matter what it is, you can appreciate it more.

After I found out that I wasn't going to die, I was able to tell my wife and my parents. My wife didn't act upset that I didn't tell her. I think she asked me how I was able to live with it all by myself. I think I just told her it would have been a lot more miserable for me to have everybody moping around. I have a lot of confidence in my wife, and I think if I had died, I would have wanted my children to have a father and I told her that. I think that she loves me and would not want me to die, but I think she would be very realistic and I would want her to remarry.

*   *   *

I have thought about what would happen if they told me I can't take any more Prednisone. For some people it has bad side effects and is very dangerous. I don't know what it would do to me to be back on the old schedule again. You know, it's funny, we are supposed to learn from our experiences, but this was such an unusual experience and I guess it can be different each time. I don't know what I'd do. I'm not going to say I would be so brave; I might turn out to be a crybaby over it. I don't know.

I still look in the mirror every day when I wake up. I still have some of it; if you look closely in my eyes, you'll see they're off-white, not white. I look at that every day and think about it, but I'm not preoccupied with death; I am preoccupied with the more commonplace and banal problems that we all have.

I still think about how lucky and very happy I am—happy to be alive. I don't mean to say that I look at life through rose-tinted glasses; some days I'm not so happy and would be a lot better off dead. I get aggravated over things; I get depressed. Like everybody else, I have my ups and downs.

*   *   *

I almost died one other time. I had meningitis when I was a little boy. I didn't know that I was supposed to die, but my family told me that the night they took me to the hospital, when they came home and closed the front door, my picture fell off the wall. Nobody said anything. Nobody even acted as if they noticed it. My grandmother just picked it up and put it back on the wall. Everybody went to bed very depressed; but I fooled them, I didn't die.

A friend of mine visited me in the hospital before I had the operation. That night we spoke very philosophically together and talked about the possibility that I had cancer and was maybe going to die. He said that he had to admit something to me; it was really bothering his conscience. I asked him what it was. He was very apologetic; he said that he was sorry that I was sick, but he was glad that it wasn't him. I told him not to be sorry. I said that if you want to know the truth, I'm sorry it's me, and I would be happier if it could have been you.

We didn't talk much after that. During the year that I thought I was dying—I never told him I was—he called me up one night and he told me he had leukemia and had about four years to live. As it turned out, it *was* him—he died a couple of years ago. It's ironic how fate plays such funny tricks on us. I think about that all the time.

Fighting Back

Bjorn Hansen, thirty-four, is a social worker for a church-affiliated adoption agency.

People do things when they think they are dying. Maybe I wanted some kind of romantic end. You know, April in Paris, watching the sun set behind the Eiffel Tower . . . thinking this is the last time I'm going to see this. I was twenty-six years old. One of my testicles had exploded in size and I was 99.9 percent certain it was cancer. I didn't go to a doctor. I just figured I'm going to die, so I decided to go to Paris.

It wasn't until I returned home that I went to a doctor. He yelled at me, saying, "You're an intelligent person, you should have known better than this. Why didn't you do something sooner?" I had no answer for him. I said I honestly don't know. I guess I just decided that this is the way it was going to be. Looking back on it, I guess it had something to do with the fact that my aunt died of cancer that Christmas. I saw what she went through—all the chemotherapy and everything else—and I just didn't want to go through with it. I wanted to let it go to the end and hopefully I would just die.

I had surgery and they removed the testicle. They thought the surgery was successful even though I had delayed it. It turned out it wasn't. I was fine until about a year later when I started getting a swelling along my rib; it was about the size of a banana. They took a biopsy and it was the same cancer that had metastasized. Over the next three years I had something like thirteen or fourteen tumors in various parts of my body. As soon as they had it under control in one place, it popped up someplace else. They told me that my chances were not so good, but they always held out hope. They didn't give me a time schedule . . . it was not like you see in the movies; you know, hey, you got two months to live.

When things were just about at their worst—they were working on four tumors at the same time—my doctor had a talk with me. He was very clinical and he had a hard time dealing with it. He had the bedside manner of a Sherman tank. He told me that things didn't look very good. I don't remember how the discussion went exactly, but when it came around to the topic of my death, he said to me, "Well, we're all going to die sometime." For a second, I was stunned. So all I said was, "Yeah, I know we're all going to die some day, nobody's immortal, but we're talking about a fairly imminent danger for me."

After three years of going at this, all of a sudden the reoccurrences stopped . . . knock on wood. My understanding is that if you have had no reoccurrences for five years, you're okay; but it is a little nebulous when you've had so many reoccurrences in the past. Also, because of all the radiation that I've had, I'm probably going to be, at one point or another, a great candidate for leukemia. So I'm in a kind of limbo.

I'm not a person who expresses anger, so I don't really know if I'm angry about it or not. I can't find the stages which Kübler-Ross describes. I couldn't relate to her book at all. I never said, "Why me." The thought never occurred to me . . . it just happened, and that was kind of it. I guess I never really believed myself to be at the ultimately terminal state where there is no hope. I'm one of these people who take two aspirin and the headache goes away by the time I've swallowed them. I never really dealt with the feelings that I had when I was in the midst of this because I was just battling. I'm a stubborn son of a gun . . . I was just going to get well and I believed it.

If somebody had told me before all this occurred that what did happen to me was going to happen, I would have said, If it did, I'd kill myself. I would blow my brains out and not go through with it. But when it did happen, suicide was the farthest thing from my mind. I think in the beginning I felt this would have a greater effect on my life than it has. I think it has had a minimal effect. It was really not much more catastrophic than a lot of other things that happen in life.

I think I'm probably where I would have been at my age regardless of what has happened. It was dramatic for me at the time, but I don't want to over-dramatize it. Besides, people don't want to hear about other people's illnesses—"organ recitals." I don't think that it was an overwhelming thing or a magical or significant event. The word cancer conjures up such terrific frightening things. It is really not at all that frightening. It's an illness, not a curse.

I don't think of myself in terms of having a terminal illness, nor do I think of myself as being miraculously cured either. It's really immaterial. Basically, I'm an optimist. I consider that I'm living a completely normal life. After all this time, I think I would find it devastating if it should reoccur. I can still become panicky at times; you have your moments when you wonder when the end is going to occur.

I think it's inevitable that I'm not going to live to be ninety-nine; but on the other hand, I might live to be ninety-nine. Right now, I'm not terminal, not any more than anybody else is. My chances are probably higher, but maybe not. I wasn't supposed to survive the last bout, so who knows?

The Facts of Life

Jack Templeton,* fifty-five, and Betty Templeton,* fifty, own and operate a small real estate agency.

JACK: I have a life-threatening illness, but it's not going to interfere with my life until it kills me. I'm scared to death of the cancer, but suppose I'm not here tomorrow? It won't make the slightest bit of difference to me, so why should I get grey hairs worrying about something I have no concern with. I'm not particularly concerned with talking about the past or the future. I'm too concerned with today to dwell on yesterday or give much credence to tomorrow. It's now that you're living.

There are people who are mentally crippled by the thought that the disease they have is going to kill them. The disease is interfering enough with your life as it is, why let it interfere more? I try not to sit down and worry myself to death, because I'm going to die soon enough anyhow. I'm not going to speed up the process, and I'm not going to sit in some corner, suck my thumb and wait for it to happen. I'm going to live until I die.

A lot of people don't understand me when I say death is a fact of life. They want to avoid that fact; they don't want to believe it. I don't think anybody gives any thought to the fact that they're going to die until maybe when they're faced with it themselves. But everybody has to go sometime, so therefore it's a fact of life and you have to live with it.

We're all running downhill, but I'm running at a pretty good clip. Learning to live with it is just a normal occurrence. It doesn't come easy to me; it's a constant struggle and I have to work at it. I have some rotten days, but it can be a beautiful lousy day. You just have to work at it. It's a great life. You can either take the time to live it to the fullest or fall by the wayside.

I could sit and wait to die, or I could go along and conduct normal everyday business. It makes me more want to keep that front door open and keep doing what I'm doing. If I was independent as far as finances are concerned, I don't know what I'd do. Everybody has romantic ideas about travel to exotic places and things like that . . . I don't know if I'd close that front door or not. . . . Nah, I might just sit here and do exactly what I'm doing. I don't know, what's there around the corner which isn't right here?

I've reached the level of my own incompetence, although I didn't realize that for a long time. I wanted to strive to get better and better, bigger and bigger; but I've come to realize it's not really necessary.

Anybody who goes into the sales business gets indoctrinated right off the bat with the idea that time is money. Money is *an* answer—you've got to pay your bills—but it's not necessarily *the* answer. I'm a good neighborhood real estate broker. I'm never going to be president of the Real Estate Board, and I'm never going to own million dollar real estate investments. I'm just going to provide a good service for the people and try to do my job right.

I just recently had another biopsy of the tongue and there's no additional growth, but the lump on my neck is still coming back and I'm waiting on the report. They may have to cut away part of my neck and face. If they take away my appearance and I have to go around with half a face, I can no longer operate my business. I'm not going to sit down and brood about what may or may not happen.

I'll handle it when it comes, so why worry about it, now. I know I have to shovel that sidewalk when it snows, but I don't have to give it any thought now.

I'm a great believer in attitude being ninety percent of the battle. I'm not trying to think myself better, but attitude can either make you or break you—your attitude can put you in the grave.

My illness is a very small part of my life. What is important in my life is life, and I'm going to live it to the best of my ability in the allotted amount that God has given me. I don't know how long that will be. All I have to be concerned with is the next twenty-four hours.

I'm trying to think myself to accept God's will. I had a good religious upbringing, but when you get away from your parents and get out into the world you start losing a lot of what your parents taught you. You get it back when it becomes necessary. It's the old story: there are no atheists in foxholes.

I'm not an evangelist or reformer, but I am concerned with my spiritual well-being and my relationship with my God. If I don't have that, I don't have nothin'. Every day I get up and ask for strength. I feel it comes from a higher power. I can take no credit; I don't profess to take any. I may collapse, spiritually and mentally, in the next five minutes, but I'm not going to give up until that time. I cannot afford to . . . there's not enough of that time left.

*   *   *

I have tasted death before. My first wife was terminally ill with cancer for two and a half years. During that period of time my sister died, my mother died, my mother-in-law died and my father died coming home from my mother-in-law's funeral. You have to go on.

I know one woman whose husband has been dead for about fifteen years. Since that time, all she is doing is waiting to die so she can join him in heaven. That's a terrible waste—just to be sitting, waiting. When my wife died, I felt a terrible emptiness. After the funeral, all the people came up to me in the cemetery with tears, saying, "Oh, Jack, what are you going to do?" I told them, "I'm going to live."

I feel I've been doubly blessed. I not only had a good marriage for thirty-three years, I now have had a good one for five and a half months and we're working on thirty-three years.

BETTY: We met through this group for widows and widowers; I felt that we were more or less guided together. My first husband was sick for eight years before he died. Somewhere along the line I finally made up my mind that life goes on regardless. It was a long, hard struggle, but you do the best you can, and that's what I did.

I got a job and was able to take care of myself and my children. I wasn't a lonely person; I was always very active. I guess I thought I really didn't want to get involved again. When Jack and I started going together, I really did have to make up my mind as to whether he meant as much to me as giving up my freedom.

The fact that Jack had cancer was no secret to me. I thought, what difference does it really make? There's nothing to say that I won't be the first to go out the door and meet death. Why worry about it? You never know when it's going to be your turn.

JACK: We went into this second marriage with our eyes wide open. Since both of us had gone through it before, we knew what the ramifications would be if anything should happen to either of us. And if the good Lord is willing, we will go through it again.

BETTY: I don't know whether I'm gifted or not, but I do

not worry. I accept things for what they are and then go on. I feel if something happens that I can do something about, good; but if I can't, I'm not going to let it upset me. I just try and live each day as it comes along. I have lived a good bit of my life that way.

We all seem to think that we are just going to keep on going forever. I think you appreciate life more when you've had a death of someone who's very important to you. I think you view life a lot more seriously than you did before. So when Jack said, "Betty, you have to make up your mind what you want to do," I made up my mind. I felt the time we spent together is more important than what may happen.

JACK: There's no such thing—like in the fairytales—that "they lived happily ever after." Practically every marriage ends in disaster of some kind. How many people just go through life married and then they lay down and die together. They don't. But the storybooks say, "They lived happily ever after"—temporarily they lived happily ever after, but in the end, somebody got hurt. That's the nature of life.

Sudden Confrontation . . .

Muriel Kessler, sixty-three, is married and the mother of three children.

I was in my late fifties. I was alive, robust and vital; I never really thought of myself as old. I led a very active life. I figured now that the children are grown up, we'd do a little bit of living. You make plans. To tell you the truth, I never thought in terms of death—people die, but that was other people. I was in good health. Somehow it was remote. All of a sudden you are told you have cancer. It was very traumatic. To me, it was like a death sentence. You ask yourself the question, why me?

I know it's more fashionable to say agnostic, but I am an atheist. Sometimes I think it would be easier to cope with my disease if I had a religious faith. You can be more gracious about accepting death because you figure, well, it's God's will and who quarrels with God. If you have an explanation, no matter how illogical, whether it is based on truth or not, you accept it and go on from there. If you have no explanation, you don't understand, and it is devastating.

When you first find out you have cancer, there is a feeling of isolation. Nobody understands and knows what you're feeling. People have trouble dealing with it and are afraid to understand. My kids were very uncomfortable; my husband didn't say the word cancer for several years. I have friends who to this day have never said the word cancer. I know that it's not that they're unintelligent or unfeeling but they are afraid. Even though more people die from heart disease and other causes, somehow cancer is like a death sentence.

I don't use euphemisms. I tell people I have cancer and that it is metastatic. I've had people ask me, "Well, how do you know; maybe it's a mistake." I guess it almost sounds like a joke. It's ridiculous . . . after six years and going through surgery and chemotherapy and radiation treatment. . . . Some people are very indelicate and will ask, "How much time have you got?" I ask them, "How much time have *you* got?"

*   *   *

When the lump in my breast was first discovered, while I was hoping against hope that it wasn't cancer, I knew it. This was a gut feeling. There is also something in the way they talk to you. You can tell. I consider myself strong, and I told the surgeon, "Whatever happens, whatever it is, I want to know the truth." I asked him what my life expectancy would be if they operate or if they don't operate. He says, "You ask too many questions." I said, "It's my life, I'm entitled to know." He says, "I'm not God." You know, they invoke the deity.

After the radical mastectomy was performed, I was told that I was clean. I had to have radiation treatments but was told it was a preventative measure. I believed them— that's what I wanted to believe. I had been asymptomatic and was getting stronger, and I felt better. When the surgery is over, and the radiation is over, you start recovering. You start doing things. You wear your prosthesis and you fix yourself up and you smile. You resume normal, quote unquote, life: but you're never the same—*never*. You become almost like a child. Everything that you are told you believe literally . . . and then you are devastated.

One year later I found out that everything I had been

told was a lie. I found out in a very bad way. I'll never forget it. I went to see my radiologist. Usually someone would go along with me, but this time I went alone. I was standing there in his office; it was around lunchtime. He was on his way out to do some shopping or something, and he says, "It's bad, it's very bad." Just like that. I'm *standing*— I wasn't even told to sit down. So I said to him, "What is it?"

"It's back; it's cancer of the lung; it's metastasized."

A thing like that doesn't penetrate so fast, so I said, "Well, what can we do?"

"The only thing we can do is chemotherapy."

I said, "Well, how much time have I got?"

"Nobody knows, we can't be explicit, but lung cancer is brutal."

Short of saying, you haven't much time, that's what it amounted to. Then he used the trite example that I can go out and get killed tomorrow.

I became hysterical. I said, "What kind of way is that to talk to anybody—*on the run?* You don't tell a patient on your way out that things are very bad. You didn't even tell me to sit down, or wait until I was with a member of my family. I know doctors are busy people, but we are talking in terms of human life here. It isn't as though somebody has a hangnail. This is cancer that has metastasized." He thought that I was a paranoic or had flipped my lid. When I finally left, I said to him, "I have never in my life wished anybody dead, but for the way you have treated me, I hope I come to your funeral!"

There was such a total lack of consideration that it is beyond description. It's not only a question of being blunt and horrible, but he just didn't behave like a human being. This is a man who I was seeing periodically for radiation treatments after surgery. Some sort of a relationship should have developed. I mean, this isn't a patient who comes in off the streets; he knew me already for over a year. Even if he hadn't . . . I think if I brought an animal to the vet and it had cancer, he would tell me to sit down, and *then* bring me the bad news.

I thought we had some sort of rapport. As a matter of fact, he was very complimentary because I always took good care of myself. I always wore the prosthesis; I was always made up. I put up a really good front. I really was scared and all that, but I sort of whistled in the dark to give myself courage. He was very friendly, and charged exorbitant fees.

I know that medicine is not an exact science. I can understand there's more art than science to it. People make mistakes . . . but to be that callous? I don't say you have to lie to a patient or give them false hope, but you can tell a person the truth in a way that doesn't cut off all hope. Doctors are educated people and they should have command of the language.

The doctors have much to learn. They don't treat the whole person. It's getting to the point where they have a doctor for your left eye and one for your right eye. It's big business. When they start to make a little bit of money, they get corrupted. Most of the young doctors I came into contact with were really very good and they cared, but somewhere between the time they care and the time they start making money, something happens to them.

* * *

In the beginning, I felt I was a victim. I used to think of myself as being on Death Row. People used to say to me, "Why, you can live many years with cancer." And I used to say, "Sure, Caryl Chessman lived thirteen years on Death Row." Instead of making plans for living, you make plans to die. It got to the point that I wouldn't even buy a ticket to the theater because you have to buy it a few weeks in advance, and I thought by that time I might be gone. A lot of my inner thoughts start with the time I'm going to

die. I don't say it out loud, but this is sort of the preface
to all my plans; everything is conditional. You never have
the security of a healthy person. People will say, next year
I'm going to go here, two years from now, I'm going to do
this. When you have cancer, you just don't do that. You live
from day to day, week to week; when you start feeling better, month to month, but that's about it. It's a terribly
insecure feeling. Sometimes I used to say to my husband,
"Well, if I'm still around. . . ." It used to offend him, although I didn't realize it at the time, how hard it was on
him. For me, it was a defense. Sort of a macabre sense of
humor. I was trying to cover up my fear and anxiety.

At first I considered myself to be mutilated. Not that I
enjoy looking at myself now, but this is it, so what. Somebody has a crooked arm, or a crooked leg, so I have one
breast and a cavity where the other one is supposed to be.
I still have pain, but I've learned to live with it.

You can get used to a lot of things. A year goes by, another year goes by, and then another. You decide, well,
I'm just going to do what I can. And it's surprising, the
more you do, the more you can do. I don't think I bought
anything for a year after I found out the cancer had metastasized, maybe longer. Not even a piece of clothing. I figured
why should I buy a pair of shoes, I'm not going to live to
wear them out. I've worn out quite a few pair of shoes since.

*   *   *

I went to a lecture once and a man who had cancer spoke.
He said cancer was the best thing that ever happened to
him. I thought the man must have had a really miserable
life if that is the best thing that ever happened to him. This
is the worst thing that ever happened to me. Nothing that
came out of it—whether it's the depth of my understanding
or the appreciation of life, my family or friends—is worth
having cancer. I don't think you acquire awareness because

you acquire a disease. The disease doesn't give you anything but trouble. Maybe it made you appreciate life a little bit more, but I doubt it. I'm not a professional patient. You see, when some people, particularly those who appear in public, start mouthing these expressions, and keep on repeating them, they start to believe it.

I have very strong feelings about the whole death and dying field. I'm not a philosopher or a sociologist. I don't try and draw conclusions, but I am a little bit skeptical when it becomes a profession, an employment, particularly when there is money changing hands. You hear a few professionals speak and they try to make you think that everything is peaches and cream. You hear them philosophize that death is beautiful. For people who don't believe in an afterlife, what can be beautiful about it—death is the final chapter; you die and you're dead. That's it. If you've ever seen a corpse, there's nothing beautiful about it. It's being alive that's beautiful.

That whole business about death with dignity—it isn't very dignified to die. I don't care if you're surrounded by all your family and you have the very best of care, what's so dignified about dying? Living is what is important. There is dignity in living. Talk is cheap, and it's very easy for these professionals to say "I care." It turns me off a little bit. While I like to be touched and embraced and all that, I don't want people to be nice to me only because I'm going to die soon.

I have no fear of death, though I don't know how people die. I haven't died yet; I don't know how I'm going to behave. Maybe I'll fight and scream and won't be as brave as I am now. I'm sure when the time comes and the pain is severe, I will be taken care of. It doesn't seem possible that in this day and age they let people suffer to a point where you wish to be dead . . . but then again, you don't know; there is a great deal of neglect in the hospitals.

*   *   *

I don't think that the way that I view life has really changed since I've had cancer. There are certain run-of-the-mill activities that you took for granted that I'm grateful for now. I'm grateful when I can put on my shoes, because there was a time when I couldn't reach my feet. When you've been independent all your life, and then need somebody to put your shoes on for you, or button you up or something, it's a little demeaning. And it takes time to accept it. I value the devotion, loyalty and care that I have received, but no matter how willingly and how lovingly the help is given to you, sometimes the people who give you that help don't understand that there is resentment in you because now you *need* their help.

As far as appreciation for life, maybe when you take a ride in the country and see the change of seasons you may say what a beautiful world it is and how happy you are to have lived to see the change of seasons. I think you express it more openly and more frequently. Not that you hadn't felt it before, but you took it for granted because you knew you were going to be here next season.

In every one of us there is a little bit of the dreamer, the poet, the pragmatic one. We are a composition of all those things and at different times in our lives these qualities come out. Values may change, I suppose; but I think the basic ones really don't. I always thought as we grew older our understanding changed and all that, but I'm beginning to believe that people really don't change that much. The way you are at seven, you are at seventy. We do change, and yet we stay the same.

I don't think my attitude towards death is really typical. I don't believe in a hereafter, and I don't worry how my body is going to be disposed of. There was a time when I thought I was going to give it to science, but after thinking about it for a while, I thought, why should I rule the roost after I'm gone, I was domineering enough during my lifetime. Whatever is going to be good for those who survive

me is what should be done. It won't matter to me once I'm
dead. It doesn't matter to me if they burn me, bury me, or
throw me to the dogs. It's now that counts.

The way I feel now is that I try to live each day the same
as anyone else. You can't pack twenty-five years of living
into one year; in one day you live one day. I didn't set the
world on fire before, why should I now? You go from day
to day and try to enjoy it, and that's all. I don't consider
myself particularly happy, but then, I don't consider
myself particularly unhappy either. You don't go through
life on a straight line—there are zig-zags. You have your ups
and you have your downs. I consider myself fairly intelligent, and I think I deal with it fairly well under the circumstances. I try to use my intelligence for living and lead as
normal a life as possible. That's the best anybody can do,
right?

I don't think as much about death as I did before. I
know that I'm not going to live my normal lifespan, but I
no longer think of myself as dying. I don't want to die,
I'd like to live to a ripe old age like Methuselah. I don't
think it's very likely. Then again, there are new drugs, new
procedures. You never really know; I never expected to
live this long. I think the word terminal is a misnomer. We
are all terminal. We are all going to die. Nobody leaves this
life alive.

Through a Glass, Darkly

Howard Greenhalgh,* fifty-eight, is the president of the Philadelphia chapter of Make Today Count, a national organization of mutual support groups for people with cancer and other life-threatening illnesses.

We are born sleeping and few of us ever awake,
unless it is upon some hideous midnight when
death startles us and we learn in grief alone what
bit of Olympian fire our humid forms enwrapped.
                                        —Max Eastman

When the doctor broke the news to me, the first words I heard—and the only ones I really remember—were cancer and leukemia. Frightening words. Indeed they are frightening words. How long was I frightened? . . . I can't say, an hour maybe. I'm not frightened; I don't fear death. I do fear dying. I think the thing that I fear the most is the indignity that is possible during those last few days. The writhing, screaming, agonizing type of thing—this I fear; but I have no fear of death at all. Absolutely none. I am certain that there is a God and a life beyond this one, and that the beauty of that life is so deep that it is indescribable. If there was anything that I feared, it was life itself. Life was more unknown to me.

*   *   *

I'm just an ordinary person. I was a salesman. For thirty-one years I had to convince people that what I was selling

67

was the best they could buy. I sold value. The more convincing I was, the more successful I was. When I was told I had cancer, my sense of values changed. I no longer cared about making money. I thought if life was just going to work every day, that's not what I want. Within three weeks of the initial diagnosis, I was out of work. I came home and I was elated. It was a feeling of joy and a release that was almost indescribable.

I thought, what am I going to do with my life? I was very confused at that point what it was I could do. I knew there were things I had to do . . . there was something, but I didn't know what it was. I couldn't define it. It was an unknown factor.

We get so wrapped up in trying to calculate life that we forget to think about it. Thinking is a privilege that most of us really do not take advantage of. What's it all about? Why are we here? What are we doing with our lives? What do we live for?—to have a nice car, a beautiful home, big money?

I don't usually quote scripture and that type of thing, but I think very often of what St. Paul said in the thirteenth chapter of First Corinthians: Now I see through a glass darkly. I daresay that people have been preaching sermons, theologians have been studying that thing for so long, but they still haven't fully explained to themselves or to the world what St. Paul was trying to say. What the theologians believe is that he was talking about the hereafter; that now we see things so fuzzy, but in the hereafter, the fog will be lifted and we will begin to see things clearly.

I like to apply what Paul has said in the "now" sense rather than in the hereafter. The point I am trying to make is that as we go through life, everything seems to be bright and vivid. We *seem* to understand, but we really don't. We do see through a glass darkly. We don't realize this until something very drastic happens to our lives. It may be a war, a depression, it may be the loss of a loved one. Probably one of the most despicable things that can happen to us in our lives is to get an incurable disease.

I saw through a glass darkly before I had cancer. I wonder if the person who just goes along and all of a sudden drops dead of a heart attack . . . people say what a wonderful way to go. Well, maybe so. But then, what a wonderful thing it is, what a wonderful privilege it is, to have some time to think—real in-depth thinking. All of a sudden, the fog is lifted. The person who drops dead of a heart attack is robbed of that.

If we have a mind to, we have the tools to permit this insight. Before I had cancer, I could see people, but darkly. Whether they were business associates or personal friends and acquaintances, they were tools to be used. I never thought of myself as a selfish person who really used people, but as I look back on it today, I certainly did. Not necessarily for financial gain, but what did I do for their lives? That question never entered my mind. That wasn't important to me.

Now, my feelings towards people are totally different. There isn't anyone I dislike, anyone I could dislike. Now I can see beyond those dislikes. It's almost like being psychic, and yet, I don't consider myself to be psychic. You see the inner souls of people, their agonies. You can see it in their eyes. You are very sensitive to their inner feelings simply because you know the vulnerability of life itself.

*   *   *

One night I was sitting alone and I did something that I was thinking about for a long time. I thought of Isaiah. When God had to get something done, Isaiah said, "Here I am, Lord, send me." I repeated Isaiah's words. That prayer can be very detrimental to your psychological well-being.

You don't utter those words unless you mean them. If you don't live up to them, it can destroy your conscience. I meant them.

Why am I here? What's it all about? As long as there's any life in my body, there's got to be a purpose in my existence; and until that life is taken naturally, then I haven't fulfilled why I'm here. It has become very obvious to me in the last few years why I'm here. At the cost of sounding boastful, I know what my life is all about. I know why I'm living. I've had my disease now for four and a half years, and I've come to realize how precious and beautiful life really is.

I am certain that there are special people in the world. They are special because they permit themselves to be used by God and the world. You won't believe how my life has been used. If people ask for help, I go. You don't question it, you don't ask for money, you go. People can take advantage of a person like that, but that person doesn't care. If you take advantage, the burden is on your back, not mine, and you'll have to answer for it.

I'm not a Pollyanna, but I won't say no to anybody or any request. That was the promise I made. I can't say no. I don't feel as though I have the right, because I'm someone special.

Without Tears

Linda Strassburger,* thirty, is an unemployed school teacher and is presently working as a bookkeeper.

I had a lump on my neck which everyone said was probably a cold or swollen glands or something like that. So I forgot about it. You know, you don't go around thinking, here comes disaster.

It didn't go away, so I made an appointment with my doctor. He decided to do a biopsy and I had the lump taken out. The terrible part of it was that it took a week to find out anything. My life was hinging on the results of that test, but the surgeon wouldn't tell me anything. My mother died of leukemia, my maternal grandmother died of cancer, and at least five or six people on my mother's side also have died of cancer. Obviously, it's going to run through your mind, but I kept pushing it aside and saying that was ridiculous.

When the results of the test were finally in, I went to my doctor with my daughter, who at the time was four. I walked in with her, and the doctor asked her if she would leave the room. He told me I had Hodgkin's disease, and he starts to cry. He said, don't throw in the towel, he was going to call in a specialist and get right on it. It was really a weird thing. I'm thinking to myself, Hodgkin's . . . that's super— he could just as well have said chicken soup. I don't know what this is; I've never heard of it. At the time, I had heard of leukemia . . . you know, the biggies.

I can remember feeling so desperate that day. It was really absurd; looking in the dictionary, not even being able to spell this. I finally found it, and what it said was: whoa, you're going, goodbye; you know, don't put a quarter in the parking meter because you're not going to get your money's worth.

I called a nurse in the family and asked her what it was. We had a lot of phone calls from the family that day, and there was a lot of crying and boo-hooing. So many things ran through my mind that day. I was not afraid of the dying part so much as I was afraid for my daughter.

They threw me into the hospital immediately. I was told that without treatment I would live two years. With treatment, well, you go five years with any cancer, and if you're still around, you can relax a little bit. They were very careful not to use the word *cure* . . . it's a possible cure. Sometimes I think if they tell you you have six months, two days, one hour or whatever, it's easier because you can plan.

I never said, "Why me?" I didn't become angry. I didn't run out every day and kiss the ground, or run out and join a convent or become a religious freak. It surprised me when people would say, "You're doing such a wonderful job; I can't believe it." I'd look at them and I'd say, "A wonderful job at what?" I've had people tell me that they would have committed suicide, that there was no way on God's earth they could have handled it; I must be very strong. Maybe I am and maybe I'm not. I try to tell people, okay, it happened, but it's not destroying me and I can accept the possibility of my death. I have to live with it.

I accepted it from the beginning. I tried to make it easier for everybody in my family. I think my main concern throughout has been my daughter. My husband is a teacher, and I decided then that in the summer when he's not working it was important for her to get as close to him as she could. I was determined not to let anything change our lifestyle at all. I still did the laundry, the food shopping. I just wouldn't let anybody do anything for me. I don't have a husband who falls all over me, and I think that's good. It saved me a lot of self-pity.

People don't know what to say to you, so they make stupid comments. I loved it when someone found out I had Hodgkin's and said, "Well, you can run out in front of a bus and get killed." That really makes me angry. That was beautiful logic for a twenty-six-year-old mother with a four-year-old daughter. Or they'll say, "Hodgkin's, I know somebody who has that and she's doing fine." You know, they'll put it down, which angers me. I'm not trying to make it something that it isn't, but don't turn around and tell me that it's a common cold. A lot of times people ask me questions. They want to know all the gory details. What is it about people, are they dying for gore? Why do people look when an ambulance pulls up at somebody's house? They may tell you that they don't want to see blood or somebody's arm hanging off, but why do they look?

The people who say they are afraid to die are really very selfish. When you die, you're dead. The people around you who survive are really the ones who suffer, not you. The only thing that scares me is the pain at the end. I've got four years behind me now, so you're supposed to be able to relax a little bit. First of all, anybody who tells you you can relax with something like this has got to be a lunatic. It doesn't prey on my mind, but there are times when I start to feel very tired or very sick, and then I start to worry. I don't like to dwell on it; it's just you can't ever get away from it. It's just a question of . . . it's something that's always going to be there. It's just up to you how you're going to handle it. I push it aside pretty much, maybe because I'm doing so well.

Maybe I'm crazy, maybe I blew it. Maybe I had a big chance to run around and do a lot of crazy things. You know, people would say, "Oh, you can excuse her, she found out she has cancer." Maybe if I walked into the doctor's and he said, "You've got a week to live" . . . so then what? I still wouldn't have money to do what I wanted to do.

I never felt desperate that I have to do this or I have to do that because next week I may not be here to do it. I honestly don't count every day any differently than before. That's a lot of baloney, because the dishes still get dirty, the supermarket is still there. . . .

The Death House

Tommy Trantino,* forty, has spent more than half his life in prison. In 1964 he was sentenced to death for the murder of two policemen. He spent nine years on Death Row before his sentence was commuted to life imprisonment. He is an artist and writer and the author of *Lock the Lock*.

> *The truth of others was untruth to me;*
> *The justice of others injustice to me;*
> *Their reasons for death, reasons with me for life;*
> *Their reasons for life, reasons with me for death.*
> —Edgar Lee Masters

The crime itself didn't matter anymore. I'm shackled, in cuffs, chains and manacles. The whole courthouse is surrounded by armed police. I'm being walked through this roped-off area into the courthouse, a contingent of cops surrounding me. The crowds of people are staring at me. They are angry, growling at me, spitting, yelling, "KILL THAT COCKSUCKER . . . MURDERER . . . COP KILLER . . . BEAST . . . MAD DOG."

They were hanging ropes in all the police stations in the state. The newspapers were calling me names—mad dog and all of this shit. They constructed this image of me that would scare Attila the Hun.

They were getting ready to kill me. To get people to kill somebody, you have to work them up. There's a whole elaborate ritual. They can't just outright murder you, there has to be some pretext for doing this. Even though people are sometimes cruel and mean, they aren't killers, they aren't beasts. I really believe that. They were putting on a show; they were having a mad dog publicity campaign. They were saying, "We'll take care of 'im, we got the mad dog in chains and we're gonna take him to the pound and put 'im to sleep."

*   *   *

I was completely demolished by the whole experience. I didn't have a friend in the world. Nothing. No lawyer would represent me; I had to use a state lawyer. Everybody believed what was being put out about me. Nobody would come near me. Other prisoners and guards were all looking at me like I was Adolf Hitler's clone.

I couldn't understand the way they were treating me. I was really trying to find some answers for why this was happening to me and why no one was helping me, but I couldn't figure it out. I could see what this was doing to my parents. I had a grandmother. She was an old woman and had a bad heart and I was worried that she would hear about it. I was so ashamed. This image that was being projected was making me suffer more than I was suffering.

They were doing all these things to me and I'm thinking, what the fuck is this, I'm not hurting anybody, I'm not acting up, I'm not resisting. If somebody asks me to do something, I do whatever they ask. Why are they doing this? I felt I was innocent of what I was being charged with. First of all, I surrendered myself to the authorities to face my accusers. I didn't assault anybody. As a matter of fact, from the time of my surrender to this day, I have not raised my hand to anyone.

I was not exactly humble to anyone; I did not back down to any of them. If somebody's going to mistreat me, I'm not going to accept that mistreatment. Even if you have a badge or a gun, you're not going to make me do what you want me to do or think what you want me to think.

I was so fucked up and depressed about this I was probably looking to get myself killed. This humiliation, this demolishment of my psyche and of my prior existence, this was all going on inside me. There was no way I could articulate that to anyone. I had a tough front which I was projecting to the outside world which scared them. I can't get angry like a normal person, you see; not me, because if *I* get angry, everybody gets frightened, 'cause they think I'm going to kill them.

I might have been a criminal or done criminal things, but that still didn't make me a mad dog. I didn't know what to do about the way I was being treated. I didn't know how to defend myself at all. I really didn't know how to help myself except by barking.

*   *   *

If someone is charged with a violation of law in this society, they're supposed to have a fair trial. That's what I read in the books. The Constitution is supposed to guarantee that; law cases that have been handed down by the courts in every state of the country say that . . . but that's not what they do.

They would rope off the courthouse and stop all activity when I came in. The whole courthouse was surrounded, inside and outside, by armed police. I would have this whole contingent of cops surrounding me. It was being projected that I was so dangerous that I needed all these escorts—and I'm supposed to get a fair trial?

When I took the stand at my trial, armed cops walked me to the witness stand. What's the jury gonna think? I'm saying I'm innocent; my lawyer is trying to say I'm crazy; and the prosecutor is saying I'm a mad dog.

There is no justice in the courtrooms. All men are created equal, equal justice under the law—it's all bullshit. They talk about these high ideals and values, and when they get people into these court rooms, they fuckin' smash them to death.

*   *   *

It is night. I'm being walked through the prison yard. The cops are up on the towers surrounding me. I'm led into a small building the shape of a shoebox. I go through one door, then another . . . they're all locked behind me. This is the death house. It's dark and dismal; it's just like being in the grave.

You are put into this box, this cage, and are told you will die at a certain time. You will be taken from your cell and have your life taken from you. There is a whole breakdown of the past. You begin to think about the whole question of your life: What did I do with my life, for my life? Why did I do this? I threw it all away—for what?

You choose the life you lead. I could blame it on a million different things, but I chose to lead a certain kind of life from childhood on that was suicidal—from dope to gangster-ism. It's easy to go on a death trip, being controlled by everything outside of yourself. That's what brought me here. All that I had been aware of consciously was to survive.

I really started to think about my life because of my thoughts of death, though I didn't stay with the thoughts of death. I said to myself, what the fuck am I doin', I'm just gonna *survive,* man? I'm jumping into this motherfucker. I'm gonna live. I'm gonna get some life outta life *in a death house.*

It's not a question of blotting death out of your mind. I was very aware that there were people who were trying to kill me, but I wasn't going to let that stop me. I wasn't going to accept it. That was my fight. I was not going to allow them to do it; I would not allow myself to do it. Just because at some point my life would cease didn't mean that

I would have to capitulate to death. I didn't have to be
frightened. I didn't have to distort my thinking. I had to
choose more carefully. I had to look at the world more
clearly.

I didn't sit down with myself and come up with all these
conclusions in one day. It was a gradual process. I didn't
think about these things intellectually, it was more an emotional response. I was shook up being put into a position
with no out. I was going out of a life that I didn't choose
to go out of. I just started thinking, I'm gonna fight death,
I'm gonna fight that inevitability as long as I can, and I'm
not gonna let forces outside of myself get in my way.

I never thought before. I knew the world was bigger
than my immediate environment and I wanted to expose
myself to the outside world. I did most of my so-called
serious reading in the death house. I never studied before
and I didn't know what the fuck I was studying, even as I
was doing it; but, man, I was really getting into things. I
got really heavy into existentialism. I wanted to think and
see what people who think are saying.

I couldn't function in this world until I knew I was a
dying man, and that made me more alive. I went outside
the death house while I was inside physically. I was thinking
how I would change my life if I was outside. Why do I have
to be a non-human person, contributing nothing to this
planet, just taking away from it, helping to kill it. I became
interested in growing. Not that I solved all my problems,
my hangups or weaknesses, but I was at least able to see
them and start working on some of the things that had
inhibited my growth. It was like a form of life that was
created in the dark.

*   *   *

The death house was gloomy, dark and dismal. There
were roaches and rats and vermin of all kinds—and the guys

became like their environment. For the most part, the guys were poor, whipped, mistreated, with no sense of worth. They had given up on life.

You were locked in your cell twenty-four hours a day. You were allowed out only once a week for twenty minutes to take a shower. There would be about ten cops to walk you down and walk you back. I thought this was a very insane place for me to be in with my present feelings about life and I started saying to myself, what the fuck is this here? You're dying anyway, whether you're in a death house or on Park Avenue. . . . Fuck it man, you're not supposed to live now? Things are gloomy, cheer 'em up, people are stupid, brighten 'em up. I had my towel, put it around my neck like a cape, and went out of my cell naked. You weren't allowed to talk to anybody, but I stopped and started talking to people anyway. The cops wound up going along with it—what were they going to do, kill me?

We had no tables in our cells. All you had was one of these army cots, and that was it. The food was garbage to begin with, and you had to eat it standing up or resting it on your bed. So I asked em, "Where's the fucking tables?" They said we weren't allowed to have them, it's a security risk. The warden came in, and I called him a motherfucker and everything else. I asked him, "Do you eat at home standing up? Why the fuck do I gotta do this?" I said, "Listen, if you don't get some kind of table or desk and a chair in here . . . you fucking get it or everytime you or anybody else comes in here, I'll fucking tear everything up and throw it out on the fucking tier."

So they got a desk and a chair for everybody. This was the start of it. I didn't tell the guys, c'mon, we gotta organize here; I did it on my own. This started stimulating the other guys: "Why don't we get hot water?" Why this, why that?

Some of the guys didn't want to do anything. Why? They might blow watching TV. So they'd accept a one-arm status as a privilege because they might lose two if they did anything. Meanwhile, your life is being taken from you, but you ignore it. I told them, "If you keep your mouth shut and just fucking lay in your bed, if you want to eat shit and live like a fucking nothing, that's what you're gonna get; but even while I'm dyin' I don't want anybody to treat me like this."

In a sense, I felt like I was a teacher. I tried to influence others. I would just open myself up to people, tell them how I thought, how I felt about things. If people have some authority over your life that is unjustifiable from a human standpoint and abuse that authority, you have a choice to remove it. I tried to show people that there are ways you can change things without hurting anyone. If someone was being mistreated, I would try to do something about it without hurting anyone, try to show people there is a way to do it. We're still human beings, and we always want to remember that; so if you get some power or control, you don't want to do to them what they're doing to you. We don't want to become the things that we are fighting against.

Guys started coming together. We started asking in very polite ways for some hot water so we could clean ourselves, so we could clean the death house. There's vermin all over the place. They would ignore us. Then we put together petitions. Gradually we had the whole death house going on strike. The law says they must keep you alive to kill you. It's an insane trip, man. Guys started going on hunger strikes.

We were making life miserable for cops and anyone who worked there or who had to come in on official business. There used to be a captain who would come in and read the death warrants. Now, there's eighteen guys in here, and you gotta hear a warrant for this one, a warrant for that one. I said, if he's gonna read this thing again, he's gonna eat every fucking word there. The bum stopped reading them.

They wouldn't let us have any recreation. The statutes say we're supposed to remain in our cells in solitary con-

finement until we're either released from the death house
or executed. We got them to change the statute. Eventually,
we even got them to change the death house to a different
wing inside the prison.

Once the warden came in and said, "Hope springs
eternal." I hated him ever afterwards . . . *hope!* You have to
have knowledge and something in your guts. You don't get
something by hoping for it, you gotta go get it. Just thinking
about a thing doesn't do it, you have to put it into practice
in some way. That to me is life.

*   *   *

I don't advocate violence, that's why I'm so against what
the prison system does to prisoners in their control. It's
easy to say I'm an animal and treat me like one. Regardless
of whether or not I'm guilty, you're saying that what I was
doin' was so bad that I should be in prison, I should be
dead, you have to take me off the face of the earth. You're
saying that I'm a criminal, I'm no good, so it's all right,
you're gonna act like a criminal to me, you're gonna do the
same kinds of things to me that I was doing to people outside.

There is nothing but violence being committed against
these men in prison. Whether it's Attica, San Quentin, Fol-
som, Trenton State, or Rahway, you have a small clique of
fucking sick bastards, who are usually perverts themselves—
alcoholics, right-wing bastards, Ku Klux Klanners—who control everything and get everybody shit scared. They utilize
the ultra-sick elements of the prison population to control
the prison. Say you had a decent superintendent or admin-
istration, they scare the shit out of them too. You're in a
state of fucking chaos all the time.

There's nothing that I can say that hasn't been said eight
billion times. Everybody knows about the prison system, but
nobody does anything serious about it. There are a lot of

people who work within the system—from prison authorities to police to judges—who I'm sure feel the same as I do.
They're not bad people necessarily, but they have no imagination, no courage to change things.

Guys rise up. You can call it revolution, uprisings, pro-
tests, strikes. They do it in all kinds of ways. Say they did
it by petition, using legal channels, or went on hunger
strikes punishing themselves just to be heard. There might
be a few newspaper articles, the public is made aware, a
few liberals may rend a garment, and a month later it's
back to the same old shit. Attica is still there and the same
people are controlling Attica who controlled it before.

It's a very strange system we live in—everybody who
preaches life they kill. Anywhere that man's oppressive
nature reigns, those who rise up and challenge that reign—
who pull on it and try to snap it, the outspoken ones, the
"instigators," the so-called leaders—are punished. They take
you away and lock you up in solitary and say you're a
"revolutionist"; or you're bought off or made crazy or killed.
It's just more open in the prisons than in the general society. The opportunity to stay in power and to perpetrate
that power, keeping people poor, ignorant and dead, keeps
others rich, fat and happy.

I and many of the men in prison refer to it as the system
of death. It's geared to kill the people it confines, and this
society allows this to occur. Not only prisoners, but whoever
works here—all who enter here die in some way. It's the
environment. You see guys that literally look like they're
shell-shocked—they look like the walking dead.

My whole attitude about cops has changed since I've been
in prison. You get to talk to cops and get to know them as
people. They have the same thoughts and feelings as you
do. You get a young guy that comes in, he wants to try and
help a little bit, he doesn't want to hurt anyone. You see
him one day, you know he's suffering, struggling, trying to
survive; you see him the next day, and all the life has gone

out of him and he's dead. You see the thing go out of him.

Within a very short time, he hates people. He might be smuggling in contraband, or busting heads. He's probably an alcoholic; his home life is in ruins. It's the fucking environment; it produces a mentality of meanness and cruelty. This just perpetuates itself and becomes embedded, and anybody who comes into this environment is gonna be victimized by it. It's not the cops' fault. Cops are just glorified inmates. They are trapped in here; they have no say about their lives; they're treated like jerks. They get furloughs every day, that's all; they let them go home. They're just in different positions, different uniforms—prisoners got khaki, they got blue . . . all in jail . . . all in jail.

People are in jails outside, too, in some sense; it's how they limit themselves. There are people outside the death house who are still in a death house. It's what they think, what they do, how they live their lives. Their job might be their death house; their home life might be their death house.

Why do some people do nothing and wait to die? People have no control over their lives; their lives seem to be rudderless. They don't do anything; they have no life of their own. That's why I think so many people are so sad and unhappy. I hate to use a cliché, but they drift like leaves blowing in the wind. They wait for this thing to come or that thing to come. They're not making choices.

Everybody dresses the same, talks the same. What is the latest fashion? What is the latest dance? How am I supposed to behave? Their lives are governed by rituals. What do they fucking do? They work all week for Uncle Sam and they go visit Aunt Sadie on the weekend . . . over and over and over again. They are living lives without life.

I see the system of death everywhere. People are breathing noxious gases all day. The fucking water they drink is full of shit. There's fucking radiation in their eyeballs and their assholes. All we have is fucking war and famine. A small number of people make all the decisions that affect the lives of everybody on this planet. It takes all your strength not to break down and cry at what's going on in the world.

I have been out of society so long that it is hard to see some things, but I think people are sick and disgusted with the state of affairs in this society. Most people don't believe that there is an alternative to the shitty world that they've been brought up in. They sit on their asses and do nothing.

I believe that people can change things, and you don't have to hurt anybody in the process. I know that this is true; all my involvement in prisoners' rights is based on this. If you speak the truth, and really believe in what you're doing and your purpose in doing it, and put your whole self into it, you become greater in every way for it. Your intellect becomes stronger, your feelings become purer. You're no longer avoiding things, pretending or bullshitting. I have been chained up in enough prisons, in the worst conditions in the world, and I know this is true: people who are supposed to be the most horrible psychotic criminals will do the right thing, the just thing, the good thing, if they are shown there are alternatives.

                    *   *   *

Having spent all that time on death row, people always ask me, "How does it feel; how does it feel to know you're going to die?" I think that is a question that any person with any kind of thinking capacity has to ask themselves. I believe most people avoid that question, and that affects their behavior and way of looking at everything in life. It's too hard to deal with, so people just stop frozen, numbed out. They are afraid to think, to make choices. They have all kinds of ways of not dealing with it, so they don't have to fight for freedom, fight for life.

When I was in the death house, you could see the electric chair if you opened a little peephole when you came out of your cell for your weekly shower. I cursed it, I spit at it, I said it wouldn't get me, that I would beat it. The other guys felt it was better not to look. They were superstitious. Some wouldn't even acknowledge it. Guys talked around it. No one would talk about death directly. That is probably the dirtiest word of them all. It was cosmetized in a million different ways.

The same thing's true on the outside. Everybody's gonna die, they just don't know when or how; but they don't allow themselves to face that reality. I think the thought of death, what it means, is too frightening. They tell their children, "Oh, don't be frightened, let me tell you about the afterlife. People die and they go to heaven, and they lie around on clouds and they smoke joints all day." That's probably what they tell kids today. The parents are frightened and they pass it on to their kids, and this distorts kids' thinking and perpetuates the myths.

All these myths, fantasies and superstitions help to control people, and people allow themselves to be controlled by these means. Most people do not think; most people are not allowed to think. They are told they are too stupid to think, so they accept the big lie. The real problems that mankind faces regardless of your interpretation of reality, are not being dealt with.

There is no afterlife. Death is inevitable; that's it. Man is mortal and goodbye. Understand it, adjust your life to it, and go on from there. As I'm sitting here, I might get a heart attack, lightning may strike me, a plane may fall out of the sky, any fucking thing. I'm not going to worry about it. What I'm saying is that it's there. I don't like it, I hate it, but I'm not going to capitulate to that hate; I'm not going to walk around sullen and forlorn. I'm not going to cop out to life. Before I die, I'm gonna live, and I'm gonna take every opportunity to live more fully. I may die in the process . . . or I may die in my bed tonight.

What you choose to do with your time is the essence

of your whole existence. I don't think you can be free, or you're really living, if you don't stay on your own clock. This is a really difficult thing to do because of the way things are in this world. There is always somebody fucking with your clock, so a lot of clocks stop before their time. I will look for whatever way is best to live and be on my own clock—not on someone else's—regardless of the condition I am in. That is why I fight for life.

It makes no difference if you're a janitor or if you're an Einstein; you came the same way, and you're going the same way—hello and goodbye. It's what happens in between that counts. What if you are the janitor, you are every bit as important as Einstein and I will try to make you see that you are. You are alive; enjoy your life, get some pleasure out of life, feel good about yourself . . . Get up and do something . . . because you're going to die anyway.

3

Two Widows

CHILDHOOD IS THE KINGDOM WHERE NOBODY DIES

*Childhood is not from birth to a certain age and at a
     certain age
The child is grown, and puts away childish things.
Childhood is the kingdom where nobody dies.*

*Nobody that matters, that is. Distant relatives of course
Die, whom one never has seen or has seen for an hour,
And they gave one candy in a pink-and-green striped
     bag, or a jack-knife,
And went away, and cannot really be said to have lived
     at all.*

*And cats die. They lie on the floor and lash their tails,
And their reticent fur is suddenly all in motion
With fleas that one never knew were there,
Polished and brown, knowing all there is to know,
Trekking off into the living world.
You fetch a shoe-box, but it's much too small, because
     she won't curl up now:
So you find a bigger box, and bury her in the yard, and
     weep.*

*But you do not wake up a month from then, two
     months,
A year from then, two years, in the middle of the night
And weep, with your knuckles in your mouth, and say
     Oh, God! Oh, God!*

Childhood is the kingdom where nobody dies that matters,—mothers and fathers don't die.
And if you have said, "For heaven's sake, must you always be kissing a person?"
Or, "I do wish to gracious you'd stop tapping on the window with your thimble!"
Tomorrow, or even the day after tomorrow if you're busy having fun,
Is plenty of time to say, "I'm sorry, mother."

To be grown up is to sit at the table with people who have died, who neither listen nor speak;
Who do not drink their tea, though they always said Tea was such a comfort.
Run down into the cellar and bring up the last jar of raspberries; they are not tempted.
Flatter them, ask them what was it they said exactly
That time, to the bishop, or to the overseer, or to Mrs. Mason;
They are not taken in.
Shout at them, get red in the face, rise,
Drag them out of their chairs by their stiff shoulders and shake them and yell at them;
They are not startled, they are not even embarrassed; they slide back into their chairs.

Your tea is cold now.
You drink. it standing up.
And leave the house.

—Edna St. Vincent Millay

In the Midst of Life

Carolyn Holmes, forty-seven, is a librarian. She has been widowed for one year.

Bob was never sick a day in his life. In the twenty-eight years that we were married, he never had a sore throat, never had a cold, never had any kind of sickness. He truly never *ever* was sick. One day he said, "Gee, I've got a headache." He put his hand behind his neck and rubbed the back of his head. It troubled him because it was so unusual; he didn't know what a headache was. He never had a headache in his life.

The headache never went away, and after several days we both began to worry. We pretended to each other that we were not so concerned . . . we weren't good at pretending. We finally went to a doctor. We hoped he would find high blood pressure or something that might explain this, but he checked him out and found nothing wrong, which was more frightening than if he had.

I began to read everything I could about headaches. Each day I would come home after having done my research and would tell him what I had learned. We discussed the subject over martinis most nights. There was always one hundred precent communication between us. As I was reading, I became worried over the possibility of a tumor, though I did not say to him that I'm worried sick you have a tumor. I emphasized each evening that since there were no other symptoms, it couldn't possibly be a brain tumor.

The headache didn't go away, and the doctor recommended a brain scan. Before Bob went for it, he had a terrible experience at work. He looked down the hallway and
everything began to sway. Later that night, he said, "I think
I'm not walking right." There was the symptom that we
were maybe half looking for. It was a terrifying moment.

I called the doctor immediately and explained there was
this new symptom. He said, "There is a definite neurological
dysfunction." Body blow! Pow! He said, "I want to put him
into the hospital at once to do the brain scan." He said,
"Don't jump to conclusions at this point, we can't be sure
it's a tumor."

Now the word was in the air and we were using it. The
terror is very difficult to put into words. There was a feeling
of things being totally out of control. Just the very word
brain tumor was frightening and terrifying.

That night I didn't show the terror . . . it was too deep
to be shown. Bob was obviously distraught. I was trying to
think of things to calm him down, but there really wasn't
anything I could say that would help. I was not about to
say, "Buck up, it's nothing," because obviously we knew it
was something. We talked about it very openly. I never said,
I'm sure it's not a brain tumor. I was not about to pretend,
and there was a chance that maybe it was. We drank too
much that night and for many nights.

*　　　*　　　*

We didn't sleep. In the morning Bob was admitted to
the hospital. He had a roommate, so we didn't stay in the
room. We found a quiet corner and we were just hanging on
to each other and waiting. It was a terrible time.

After the brain scan was completed, my family doctor
approached me and I knew it was time to get the word.
He was very ill at ease; he could not meet my eyes. He was
a quiet man and not very good with people. A good doctor,

but not the kind who would be good at this type of thing. He said, "Well, there is a lesion," and there was the terror again. I said, "What is a lesion?" He said, "There is something in his brain. Maybe . . . probably . . . a tumor." He quickly added that it was in a spot that he thought could be operated on. That is a moment I will never forget. I just went to pieces right there in the corridor. I really can't describe it, just absolute terror. The whole world just stopped and smashed into twelve million pieces.

The neurologist spoke with me a little later. By that time I had collected myself; I was in control of my emotions. I was not going to cry anymore. Somehow, I put on the old social front. The poor guy didn't know how to handle it; he was terrified that I would fall apart. He was so acutely ill at ease, that I tried to put him at ease. I said, "Don't worry, I'm all right." He explained the best he could what the situation was; that there was a lesion and it was probably a tumor. I remember wondering how long Bob would have to live and not asking. I asked if it was malignant. He said he couldn't tell until we operate. He asked who my surgeon was. I had a wild desire to laugh—who was my *surgeon?*

Later, I resented the fact, and I still do a bit, that I had to calm him down, that there wasn't a person in the hospital to whom he could have gone and said, "I have to tell a patient and his wife that he has a brain tumor. Emotionally, I need help myself with this. Come with me and help me with this situation."

I went into Bob's room and we simply wept. There were no words . . . there was nothing to say. A lot of thoughts were racing through my mind: If Bob dies, how can I possibly go on? How could the world go on without Bob in it? I couldn't imagine living without him. The thought of Bob not being alive was unbearable. I have never been as frightened in my life . . . far more frightened than when he was actually dying.

We were both just hanging on to each other. We were really just knocked silly by it. How could his happen? What could we do? Bob was an extremely practical man, a go-to-the-heart-of-the-matter-and-do-something-about-it man. He said to me, "This is the first thing in my life that I can't do a goddamn thing about. I can't control it."

I don't remember any pretense of any kind on either of our parts, but I do remember a lot of jumbled feelings. We tried to find some hope that maybe it wasn't malignant, but we thought benign was a sort of a miracle and not very likely. I think I thought the worst because a brain tumor to me meant probable death, and I'm sure Bob thought the same.

The next day, we had to go to another hospital for further tests to have the diagnosis confirmed. This had to be done at once. The tests indicated there were probably many lesions. Bob looked fine at this point, and there was no pain. He said, "This is an awful thing to have. The poor young nurses would ask me what are you in here for, and when I say a lesion in the brain, it gets everybody upset."

We contacted a surgeon. Bob made it clear that he wanted to be told the truth. The surgeon explained it could be one of three things: It could be a secondary site tumor, which would mean there was a malignant tumor that had metastasized, and the tumor in the brain was feeding from another source, in which case there was absolutely nothing that could be done. It could be a primary site tumor which grows on the brain. We could treat it with radiation and chemotherapy, but in the long run there is nothing that can be done. A person with this kind of tumor can live a year or two and be in pretty good shape. The third possibility is that it could be benign. I hoped and prayed that it was benign, but I immediately thought it was the first one. Bob and I talked about it, and he said he would like to go home first and get his affairs in order.

*   *   *

It was a nightmare of a week. When we came home Bob went right to the liquor cabinet to mix drinks. We just sort of sat right there on the floor, grabbed hold of each other, and went to pieces again. We drank too much and just absolutely went to pieces. How could this be happening to us?

Every day for eight hours a day Bob went over all his papers. He was very worried about whether I could handle the finances, and more importantly, would I be all right. This was his consuming obsession. Each night, we would stop working about five o'clock and head for the liquor. Each night we had filet mignon. I didn't care what he did or how much he drank; I hoped he would get absolutely blotto. Whatever he wanted, he was going to have. All I wanted was for it to be our week . . . nothing else mattered.

*   *   *

We finally got the word that Bob could enter the hospital for surgery and we drove up to that amazing, grim, forbidding building. Once we were there, some of the terror began to leave. Things were beginning to fall into some kind of pattern. We were not being buffeted around any longer. We were on some kind of a path, and we just took one day at a time.

The operation took place four days after we entered the hospital. I just lived there day and night. We were terribly eager to get going—it's terrible to wait for an operation. During the time we spent there, there were some black moments, but more peaceful ones. We talked about the possibility that Bob had a secondary site tumor and asked the doctor how long he would have in that event. He said a couple of months.

Bob said to me, "If it goes pretty well and I feel comfortable for a couple of months, is there anything we could be doing that we had never done?" I said, "Gee, I can't think of a thing." Then he said, "We've had a hell of a life together." We had a good laugh over it.

When they operated they discovered it was a secondary site tumor and that there were multiple tumors that had metastasized in the lung. Bob had lung cancer which had not shown up on any x-ray. It was probably caused by his work in chemistry all his life; he was probably a victim of industrial cancer.

After the operation, Bob had trouble sleeping and was very frightened in the middle of the night. He would say something is wrong. This feeling of disorientation never left. The tumors literally raced; he deteriorated rapidly. In a primary site tumor, one by one, all the functions that the brain controls are lost over a period of six months to two years. It is absolutely hell to watch. We were spared that, except everything that usually happens in the case of a primary site tumor happened to him in one week. I spoke to the doctor about this terrible deterioration and asked him to take Bob off any medication that would artificially preserve his life. We had twenty-eight years together—we didn't need a couple of lousy months.

*   *   *

His brain ruptured two days before he died. I don't know what one feels when their brain ruptures. He had no mind left at all, but he would pick up a pillow or a glass of water and say, "Where is the accuracy." He would restlessly walk up and down the room and say, "Where is the accuracy." I think this was a significant statement for him. Control was a terribly important thing for him, and this was a situation he could not control. If he could find the "accuracy," he could get control again.

We went through two very peaceful days. It was as if we had been through every emotion since the beginning and little by little I was beginning to accept it. I think the way one grieves has a lot to do with the way one's beloved dies. With a heart attack out of the blue, it would probably have manifested itself differently, but by the time his brain ruptured, I was just praying that it would end soon.

Those two days we simply played games. Bob was absolutely incoherent, but he seemed to know me and called me by my name. He saw somebody walk past the door and thought it was a waiter. I would pretend that we were out to dinner. I filled a glass of water and said, "Here's your martini," and he would drink it and think it was a martini. I went through a whole menu with him. I'd say, "What would you like to have? Would you like the flounder stuffed with crab?" It was a very happy time; a peaceful time.

Bob had a seizure and went right into a coma. He died twelve hours after that. I sat with him and I held his hand that day. It was a very calm time. I went home about eight o'clock knowing he would probably die while I was gone.

The phone rang about 12:15. It was the doctor. He said Bob had died . . . and I remember saying, "Thank God."

Oglesby

Muriel "Goldie" Oglesby,* fifty-two, is a poet. She has been widowed for a year and a half.

The doctor asked her what she wanted done
With him, that he could not lie there many days.
And she was shocked to see how life goes on
Even after death, in irritating ways;
And mused how if he had not died at all
'Twould have been easier—then there need not be
The stiff disorder of a funeral
Everywhere, and the hideous industry,
And crowds of people calling her by name
And questioning her, she'd never seen before,
But only watching by his bed once more
And sitting silent if a knocking came . . .
She said at length, feeling the doctor's eyes,
"I don't know what you do exactly when a person
*   dies."*

—Edna St. Vincent Millay

I had just been divorced. I had taken an apartment and three months later Bill (or Oglesby, I never really called him Bill) moved in next door. Neither one of us ever wanted to go through another marriage. We had two unfortunate ones between us, you know, and well . . . We were married a year later. It was the most beautiful marriage in the world. I think after you've had a bad experience or a bad marriage—like Frank Sinatra says, "The Second Time Around"—you appreciate more the beauty and wonder of happiness.

Shortly after we were married, Oglesby began to get angina attacks; he had a very high pressure job. In January he had a minor coronary. We had made our retirement plans and we were going to move to Colorado to a place about 13,000 feet high where the air is pretty thin. The doctor suggested a test for altitude. Oglesby didn't pass the test and the doctor advised us to have immediate open-heart bypass surgery. We got to Houston, Texas, the next day and checked into St. Lukes Hospital. There was a sleep-in arrangement—unless the wife was the one giving the man the heart attack. There was no thought of death whatsoever, never thought of it at all. We were just so totally happy that he was to have this operation and we would have so many more years together. Not one thought of . . . we were like a pair of honeymooners in the hospital.

The night before the operation Dr. Cooley—who is a very famous heart specialist—came to see us. He said to me, "Goldie, go out and buy yourself a new dress. You will be dancing in ten days."

The operation was slated to go up 6:30 in the morning. There were ten men all having the same sort of by-pass operation that morning and he was cheering everybody up. I went right up to the operating room door with Oglesby; he sat up in the stretcher, we kissed and he said, "See you in a little while, hon." I told him to behave himself.

I went back to the waiting room to sweat it out with the other wives. I was the only calm one there and was consoling and being "Miss Pollyanna" to every other uptight wife, mother, or sister who was there. No thought . . . I mean my Oglesby was indestructible.

Oh, it was about a half-hour later and I happened to look up; Doctor Cooley was standing in the doorway of the waiting room with tears streaming down his face. I looked at him, he nodded . . . Oglesby was dead.

It's hard to remember exactly, I think a sort of numbness set it—like total shock. I was told afterwards, and felt it quite a few hours later, that I had slammed my hand against the wall. In fact, I had broken my little finger, which has never been set. I wouldn't let anybody touch me. I think I was the only one there who didn't cry.

I had to see for myself that this wasn't just a nightmare. I remember they allowed me in to see his body, which was a horrible thing—there had been some mistake and they hadn't cleaned his body. He was covered with blood, the sheets were bloody and he was just lying there. The only really vivid thing I remember is that I grabbed him and sort of pulled him up and was shaking him and saying, "Honey, this is no time to play jokes on me; c'mon, we got things to do." I couldn't believe that Oglesby would go anyplace without me—we even went to the supermarket together. This was the first time he didn't do what I asked. . . . He didn't even answer me.

*   *   *

I made the necessary arrangements and calls. I had to call his family of course; he had a sister and brother, and his mother was living in Denver. They wanted him brought to Denver for burial because of his mother; that wasn't my wish, I wanted him closer to me. I called my daughters, and one of them got on a plane immediately and arrived in Houston later that night.

I went back to my hotel room. I asked the switchboard operator to screen all calls unless they identified themselves as family—I had been getting calls from priests and other well-meaning people. People were trying to be nice. The hotel sent a dinner tray up, which I didn't eat. I didn't eat for weeks and dropped fifty pounds inside of two months; food would not go down. All of the other men who had the same operation that morning and were in worse condition than he was, survived. Their wives tried to come in and see me. I just told them I wanted to be alone.

I was thinking of crazy things: What do you wear to a funeral? I hadn't planned on going to a funeral. Will Oglesby be on the same plane with me? I remember thinking, Goldie, you love this man so much, how come you aren't crying? My eyes were perfectly dry, I couldn't come up with an answer.

I think I just happened to sit at the desk. There was this empty piece of paper with Holiday Inn scribbled across the top—you know, every hotel room has a little portfolio, hotel stationery and so forth. I started to write; I was like a robot. I wasn't thinking, just doing everything automatically. When I stopped, I walked away and completely forgot about it. It wasn't until later when my daughter arrived and saw the piece of paper that I realized I had written a poem.

About six o'clock the next morning we went to Denver. I stayed at my sister-in-law's until the funeral was over. I was there anywhere from three to five days. I was in shock and really not even sure of time. A doctor prescribed sleeping pills and my sister-in-law insisted I take one every night. I allowed only the immediate family to view the body and then insisted that the casket be sealed—that was not my Oglesby lying there, he would have never wanted anyone to see him looking like that.

I still wasn't crying; it took me a long time to cry. I left Denver immediately after the funeral. There they do it in a peculiar way. After the services, the pallbearers take the casket out and the family does not go to the graveside. Oglesby is in his Rockies where he wanted to be. I have never seen his grave.

*   *   *

I came home and just couldn't stay in the house any longer. I called a friend and asked her to find out if she could get me an apartment immediately. When I first moved there and went into a strange bedroom with a single bed, it suddenly hit me; the dam broke loose. I spent most of my time sealed off in my room alternating between crying and writing. Never having written anything before, death was sort of a catalyst that had released this in me.

I got very little sleep. I would sort of catnap, then get up two, three o'clock in the morning and suddenly find myself writing out a poem. When I got that out of my system, I would doze off for a little more. I did wallow in self-pity; I'm not ashamed to admit that. I don't feel guilty; it's really a very normal thing. Nothing seemed to penetrate through to me logically or rationally. I was encased in a transparent shell.

Oglesby and I were both past the child-bearing years— well, I was anyhow. Sometimes we would say, why couldn't we have met at least ten years earlier. What a beautiful child the two of us would have raised. I began to think of the poetry as our children—mine and Oglesby's—children that were conceived in death.

I withdrew completely and avoided people as much as possible. I couldn't talk about it without a quiver in my voice and I didn't want anyone to see me like that. Oglesby used to call me his skinny Totie Fields, a real comedian. This was the façade I wanted to continue. I didn't want to impose my grief on my daughters or my friends. They give you a couple of weeks of sympathy and then they don't want to hear about it anymore; you know, life goes on and they have their own problems too. The world doesn't revolve around me, the *"widow."*

I was hostile; there is no other word for it. I mean, why me, who did I hurt? You have to cope with loneliness, you have to cope with all sorts of . . . it seems that even inanimate things act hostilely towards you. Oglesby was in federal service; therefore you had all that bureaucractic sit-and-wait nonsense to contend with—paper after paper to fill out and then get lost in the mail, and then you redo the whole damn thing again. My affairs weren't settled for quite a few months and I was becoming very angry with the world.

*   *   *

We all go through these crazy periods of numbness, shock, anger, depression; you come up with unrealistic goals which are impossible to obtain. You've got to go one day at a time and cope with that one day—it may be a beautiful day, today I had a good one, or it may be a bad day. Believe me, these bad days come less and less and you are able to cope with them better. You've go to realize it's normal— you'd be abnormal if you didn't have a cry-day.

There is one important aspect I would want women especially to know, and that is preparing for the eventuality of the death of a partner. Women outlive men. People don't want to talk about it, but they have to—it's a necessary thing. As hard as it is going to be, it's an important part of living. Many times Oglesby would try to sit down with me and say, "Look Goldie, something may happen and I want you to do this or that." I would say I don't want to hear it, I refuse, and walk out of the room. I wouldn't listen and that was wrong—that was terrible.

Sit down and discuss it, talk about insurance, tell your wife where you keep certain papers, talk about how and where you want to be buried. As hurting as it can be at the moment, it saves you a lot of grief later. As unfortunate as it may seem, there are financial aspects of death to consider. I didn't even know how to reconcile a bank statement— I mean I would go into instant hysteria when the statement came—I had no idea; the bank had to teach me. We had a joint checking account, and to me joint was Oglesby put in and I wrote. I had no business experience—really an Edith Bunker dingbat mentality—no idea of the value of money.

If anything I could say can help somebody else, great;

but in the final analysis, nobody can tell someone the how-to's and how-not's of being a widow. It's a personal experience of aloneness that each person has to solve by themselves in their own way.

*   *   *

The Christmas just prior to Oglesby's first heart attack I had two portraits painted as a gift for him. I don't know where they are now. My daughters took the photograph album and all the pictures. I told them I wasn't ready to face that. I'm beginning to feel that I want to see the pictures again. I think that maybe this summer I will visit Oglesby's grave. Right now, I don't think it would serve any good purpose; I don't intend to become a grave-sitter; everything I have to say to him I've said in my poems.

I am not hostile about it anymore. I am able to meet the world and speak to people without a quiver in my voice or impose my grief upon them. If I have a bummer day, I lock myself in my room, attack my typewriter and get it out of me. Then I am ready to go back into the world.

I am slowly reinvolving myself. I've faced the fact that dead is dead and I am able to accept Oglesby's death. In fact, I think I am a lucky widow. He never had time to suffer and he didn't vegetate. Oglesby lived a man and he died a man. That's a beautiful thought.

4

The Rites of Passage

CONDOLENCE

They hurried here, as soon as you had died,
Their faces damp with haste and sympathy,
And pressed my hand in theirs, and smoothed my knee,
And clicked their tongues, and watched me, mournful-eyed.
Gently they told me of that Other Side—
How, even then, you waited there for me,
And what ecstatic meeting ours would be.
Moved by the lovely tale, they broke, and cried.

And when I smiled, they told me I was brave,
And they rejoiced that I was comforted,
And left, to tell of all the help they gave.
But I had smiled to think how you, the dead,
So curiously preoccupied and grave,
Would laugh, could you have heard the things they said.

—Dorothy Parker

The Critic

Daniel Bernstein, forty-two, is a physician.

*Although most men lead lives bearing more resem-
blance to that of James Joyce's Leopold Bloom than
to that of Homer's Ulysses of the hyacinth beard, in
death they insist upon their heroic due. Far from
regarding that natural phenomenon—death—as the
great leveler, they have come to visualize it as the
great elevator—the one opportunity to participate
in the epic tradition . . .*
                                —Ruth Mulvey Harmer

I don't like funerals at all. It's an artificial and weird situation. This has nothing to do with being a doctor, just my
own personal feelings. To a certain extent it's important;
it's the final end. Certainly people need something more
final than the doctor coming out of a room and saying, he
just died.

I like the idea of a closed box with no viewing. I think
the person should be buried within forty-eight hours after
the death—get it over with. We make too much of a fetish
about all the trappings of a funeral. I find most eulogies re-
pulsive because most of them can't be sincere. Most people
can't face the truth.

Take a person who comes into my office with a psycho-
neurotic complaint; he's a hypochondriac and there is abso-

lutely nothing wrong with him. Let's face it, if you come out and say, "You're a hypochondriac and there is nothing wrong with you," he'll go to another doctor. You don't tell a person, "It's all in your head, go home." There is no compassion involved in that; it's cruel.

You start feeding him a line and try to give him an explanation. You try to explain away the problem in a way that makes him feel that you are interested in him and you're going to work with him to help resolve the symptoms. It's hogwash; it really is hogwash, but it's useful hogwash.

To a certain extent the funeral is useful. I think most people like it—most people need it. There is no question—people need a lot of baloney. The humdrum life of the average person is built around baloney one way or the other; but I think you have to separate useful hogwash from ridiculous hogwash.

The Undertaker's Lament

Christopher Van Doren, forty-seven, has been a funeral director for twenty-six years and owns and manages his own funeral home.

When answering the funeral home telephone, always identify the establishment and the speaker, as: "This is the Blank Funeral Home, Mr. Blank speaking." Nothing is more incongruous than a funeral director answering his telephone with a gruff "hello" or "yes" and then changing to a more pleasant tone of voice the instant he discovers that this is a death call. . . .

It should also be remembered in concluding the telephone conversation that the funeral director does not thank the bereaved relative for calling him. This would be gauche indeed.

The man in charge should introduce himself at the door and request permission to enter. It is not in good taste to use such customary greetings as "good evening," for this is not a good evening for the bereaved relatives.
—Clarence Strub and Lawrence "Darko" Frederick,
The Principles and Practice of Embalming

You know, it's funny. When a lot of people meet me for the first time and find out I'm a funeral director, they'll say, "Geez, you're always smiling. You seem to be an awful happy fellow for a funeral director. What am I supposed to do, walk around with a long, morbid face? I'm a human being, I'm entitled to enjoy life as much as the next guy. In this industry—when you're dealing with grief and death every day—if I didn't smile and keep a sense of humor, I'd wind up in a nut house.

People always say to me, "You don't look like a funeral director," and I say, "How is a funeral director supposed to look?" I guess a lot of people still have this Sam Spade, Digger O'Dell image in their minds. They have the impression that we are supposed to go around in black suits, black ties and high silk hats; you know, look half dead yourself and have a cold, clammy handshake.

You know there still are some people who think we're body snatchers, just waiting for a person to drop, and that we're all alcoholics. Even people who know funeral directors personally, when they go out socially with him they're not thinking of him as a funeral director but as a person, but I'm willing to bet that if you ask these same damn people what funeral directors are like, they'll still say drunken body snatchers.

Years ago, the funeral director was kind of a social outcast. People would talk about him, joke about him. He may have been respected for his wealth—most people think that funeral directors are wealthy; you know, he has a big black car and a fancy suit, so you figure that that guy is doing all right—but he was never accepted. People didn't want to face the reality of death and they kind of took it out on the poor funeral directors. To them, he *was* death.

I think there are a few reasons why the funeral director has been labeled as an habitual drunk. To some extent, I think it was true in the past. There is very little advertising for a funeral home. All right, how do you draw customers? You have to be friendly and go out socially and meet people. Now, the place where the old-time funeral director did most of his public relations work was in the corner saloon. He would go in, shoot the breeze with the fellows—you know, buy half a dozen rounds of drinks—and become known to everybody. So he gets into the habit of drinking.

He never could be a happy-go-lucky guy. He always had to walk around looking sad, somber; putting on a front. He was supposed to look that way. This is what people demanded of him.

Today, the funeral director's image is changing. I think now if he went to a football game with a gray flannel suit, people would tend to make fun of him. He is as much an accepted part of the community as the butcher, the clergyman, the doctor and the lawyer. He is expected to cut his lawn just like his neighbor does. He is no longer in the neighborhood bar buying drinks. Now he is active in the service clubs—the Lions Club, the Kiwanis, the Rotary— and he is active in his church.

I'm on the First Aid Squad. I don't want to sound like a ghoul, but I like to get out and drive the ambulance. I enjoy it; it's my thing. Years ago, that would be unheard of. In the six years that I've been on the First Aid Squad, I've only had one person say to me, "You've got a lot of nerve going out on an ambulance trying to find business."

There was a time when people wouldn't shake hands with an undertaker. Today, we are in demand. Service clubs, church groups, and even senior citizens' groups want us to come in and talk about death. All the taboos are gone.

You're in the limelight all the time, and you are a goodwill ambassador. Frankly, your work depends on their goodwill. There was a time fifteen or twenty years ago when no one made pre-arrangements for funerals. But today that file of pre-arrangements in the average funeral home gets bigger and bigger and bigger.

A funeral director today is proud of his profession and he is careful of his public image. It's always in the back of his mind that he has to keep up that image. He is always striving for professionalism. A doctor or a lawyer is up on the top level. When you're in second place, like Avis, you try harder.

You are very sensitive about your position. You don't go out and get rip-roaring drunk; no one likes to see a funeral director loaded. You don't make jokes about yourself or your profession. You always treat it with the utmost respect, because if you start making jokes, then people say, "Well, he thinks it's a big joke." It's certainly not a joke to them when the death occurs. The book *The Loved One** made ridicule of our profession. When someone says to you, "Take good care of Dad," they mean it. To them, that dead body *is* a loved one. You have a responsibility on your shoulders, and you *are* going to take good care of Dad.

People often make fun of funeral directors only because of their own fear of death. Everywhere a funeral director goes, somebody's got a joke. They call me "Digger," they call my son "Little Digger." A lot of people will say to me, "I hope I don't see you again," but I've got an answer for them. I'll say, "You are very fortunate when you see me. When you can't see me, then you've got problems."

In the Lions Club or the Rotary you've got people with a "wider" sense of humor, and every now and then they'll poke jibes at you, but you learn to live with it. All the jokes are stale. In the twenty-odd years that I've been around, you'd think somebody would come up with one that was original. But you just accept it, what can you do. If I go on a trip, I never tell anybody I'm a funeral director. If someone's nosy enough to want to know, I'll tell them I'm a shoe salesman or some b.s.

You go to a party that's dull. As soon as the funeral director walks in, it livens up. All of a sudden, everybody's a comedian. Everybody comes out with their little jokes, you know, somebody just heard a good one about a funeral director. It's the same old Digger O'Dell stuff: "How's busi-

* by Evelyn Waugh

ness? Dead." Oh, gosh, there's so many. "You're in the only
business that when it's dead, it's good." Stuff like that, or,
"How're things, still picking up?" Or, "I hear you've been
cutting up a lot lately." They run through the whole bit.

You know, you want to forget work. It's a twenty-four
hour job because you're on call all the time. You want to
get away from it and enjoy yourself and have a good time,
but there's no escaping it. Every conversation ends up with
the funeral business. The question that always comes up is,
"How do you embalm?" They want to know the "hidden
secret." Now, of course, they've heard all kinds of weird
stories, like the funeral director cuts them from stem to
stern and stuffs them with straw; you know, nothing short
of taxidermy. Either they heard it from a third party, or
it was something they saw in a Laurel and Hardy movie.

Every so often the little cracks come out. You get the
person who says, "Oh, don't touch me," or, "You mean
you do the embalming and everything?" "You seem like
such a nice guy, how can you do that type of work?" I was
at a party recently and I was talking to this woman. Somehow we got talking about her husband's job, and then she
asked me what I did for a living. I said, "I'm a funeral
director." She jumped out of her chair and took off and
refused to come near me the rest of the night.

You know, I still have to be careful about asking a person,
"How do you feel?" I don't dare visit somebody in the hospital unless he's a very close friend of mine; I'll send flowers
or something. I have a very good friend who is sick in the
hospital right now, but I won't visit her because I know
she's a very excitable, superstitious woman. If I walked into
her room, she'd probably think that it would put a jinx on
her or something. Years ago, I walked in on a fellow who
was an old friend; we were kids together and everything.
He was in the hospital with lung cancer. I was dying to go
down and see him. So I walked into the room and he's there
lying in bed. He's all white, skinny as hell. He took one

look at me, raised himself up and said, "You son of a bitch, what the hell are you doing here? I'm not dead yet!"

I'm even hesitant about calling anyone's house unless it's a close friend. I belong to several organizations, and once I was on a telephone committee. It was my responsibility to call five individuals and tell each one to call five others. So I called one member's house and said, "This is Mr. Van Doren, could I please speak to your husband." When he came to the phone, he was kind of leery. The next time I saw him, he said, "Don't *ever* call my house again." Every now and then, an organization like the Red Cross or the American Cancer Society will ask me to go door to door to solicit funds. As much as I hate to refuse them, I tell them I can't. If anyone sees me coming, the first thing they'll do is shut the door.

There are some people that even to this day if they see me walking down the street they'll get on the other side. You can feel the animosity. But you know you have to be an amateur psychiatrist. You're the one that buried their mother or father or husband or wife, and even though they are aware that I had nothing to do with the death, I was the one that took that person away.

Of all the removals I've been on, one in particular has stuck in my mind. It was Christmas time. The Christmas tree was up and this man passed away after a hard day's work, lying on the couch. He had six small children. Now, here you are, taking away the breadwinner to the funeral home. It's a very awkward position to be put in. I'm sure the family didn't look kindly on me coming into their home at that time.

Sometimes when families come in and make arrangements they're a little bit on the nasty side. You're usually the first person outside of close friends or family they come in contact with. They resent what's happened to them, so you're going to get the brunt of it. As with anything else, you usually don't take things out on your own family, you most likely would take them out on a stranger.

A couple of weeks ago a woman died of cancer and her daughter came in with her girlfriend to arrange the funeral. Now, this girlfriend read Jessica Mitford's book,* so she knew all about arranging funerals. The daughter said, "We don't want anything lavish, we want a very simple funeral. I don't believe in expensive funerals," and so on and so forth. So I took them into the selection room and explained the basic differences in the caskets, why one is more expensive than the other, and I let them be. The girlfriend just sat there with her mouth open, and she says, "You know, this isn't at all what I expected. I read Jessica Mitford's book and this isn't at *all* the way she said it would be." I guess she thought that I was going to push them into a solid copper whether they wanted it or not.

Now, I read Jessica's book, and there are a lot of things in the book that are true, but there are a lot of things that are not true. I'd say it was about twenty percent fact and the rest was all distorted. She had to make her book interesting so it would sell. She made a lot of money. I think anyone who does any writing has this as their main objective.

Not to denigrate our industry, but I've heard different funeral directors say that in this casket or that casket your mother would be more comfortable. When a person is dead, he's dead, and there's no way you're going to make him any more comfortable, no matter what you put him in. You should have made him more comfortable when he was alive. If a family has means and wants to spend money, fine; but nothing will make them any more comfortable—not at this stage of the game.

I would like to believe that as far as I'm concerned, I don't sell you anything, you *select* what you want. A Volkswagen will get you the same place, and just as quick, as a

* *The American Way of Death*

Rolls Royce, a Cadillac or a Porsche. It makes no difference
if you have a hundred-horsepower motor or a 250-horse-
power motor, the speed limit is still fifty-five miles an hour.
You're going to have a little more luxurious ride in a
Cadillac than you would in a Volkswagen, but you have
to pay more to ride in it. As far as the high cost of dying
is concerned, I don't think it costs anything to die. If you
want to spend $10,000 for a funeral, you can do it, or you
can be buried without a funeral for a lot less. But everybody has a tendency to want the very best for their loved
ones.

Today, burial societies are telling you that your family,
their family and the family before them are all wrong; that
there is no such thing as having God around at a service
or anything. They underestimate the public when they talk
like that. Their idea is: as *fast* and as *cheap* as you can do
it, get 'em down there. That's a lot of nonsense. These are
people that just don't want to sit up and face their obliga-
tions, that's what it amounts to. They want everything easy
in life, but God didn't want it that way. If he did, you
wouldn't get sick and you wouldn't die; it would just be
one utopia for us on earth. No-sir-ee, people don't ask to be
born and they don't ask to die, but you have these responsibilities that go along with life and that's all there is to it.
Memorial services are for the birds.

The clergy that will go out and tell families that they
don't have to spend money on funerals and think funeral
directors are the only ones they can pick on . . . well, they
are mighty mistaken. Let me put it this way. I think a
clergyman has enough to do if he does his job properly and
in a religious way—he doesn't have to go out and stick his
nose into other things—but if there is not enough work for
him . . . well, that's a different story. These people that will
approach a family and change their minds—in other words
tell a family that they haven't got a right to do what they
want anymore—at a time when their minds aren't function-

ing properly . . . that's the story that they used to hand us:
You catch people at a time when they are in sorrow and
you convince them that . . . That's a lot of baloney. A
funeral director can't convince you; he's got a casket show-
room down there and you pick what you want.

These people who want a funeral that's a little elaborate
and so forth believe that way, and that's all there is to it.
Most people know what they want before they come in because they buried in the family before. A lot of them just
come in and say, "I want exactly what Dad had," or, "I want
such and such a casket." This is their thing in life.

I'm proud of being a funeral director and the service
that I perform for the community. I like my work, though
it's not a job you really could enjoy. In a small town like
this, you bury most of your friends, so that part of it is
not so hot.

You're dealing with death every day, and you recognize
that you are mortal and it's just a matter of time. The last
two months, we just had a rash of forty- to fifty-year-olds,
and it makes you think, golly, I'm going to be dead someday
too. But you try to push it out of your mind, which is, I
guess, what most people do. I hate to make the comparison,
but just as a furniture salesman is used to seeing furniture,
I'm used to seeing bodies.

I still smoke, I'm overweight, I don't get enough exercise, I'm supposed to lay off cholesterol but I eat a few eggs
every now and then, and I like ice cream. I work on people
all the time who've had heart attacks. Knowing what I
know, I should be deathly afraid.

I guess I'm not afraid to die, although I wouldn't want an
incomplete life. I don't know what a complete life is—in
this business you bury kids. I think, though, I'm better
prepared for death than the average person. My house is in
order, my wife and children have been provided for, the
insurance is paid up. My spiritual house is in order; I have
always been active in my church.

I have a nice cemetery plot, and have made all my funeral arrangements. I'll have a day-and-a-half viewing—that means seven to nine, two to four, seven to nine. I'd like to see all the gang from all the organizations I belong to come in and view, and all my friends come in and say a last goodbye to me. I want a service, and I want to go to church. That's all I ask.

Naturally, I'm going to have the best, because if I can't get that after being in this business all these years . . . that should be one fringe benefit that I get, right?

Last Respects

Garrett Hartmann, thirty-one, is an advertising salesman.

It was the damnedest thing. I needed a job to help get me through school. I tried all the normal-type places but had no luck. So one day I tried one of the local funeral homes. I walked in off the street and introduced myself: I said that I was a college student and was looking for part-time work and that I was willing to do anything. They said they really weren't looking for somebody, but I guess they took a liking to me.

I'll never forget my first day. It was a big old house. I came in the front door; there was a sign there with little plastic letters saying that so-and-so's funeral was being held tomorow. I just said to myself, gee, there's somebody back there. Bert and Harry, the fellows that owned the home, said, "Come on back, we want to show you around." Immediately they took me back to the embalming room. Now, I've been to funerals before, but I've never been behind the scenes, so I really didn't know what to expect.

I said to myself, gee, if I blow this I'm gonna lose the job, so regardless of what's on the other side of that door, I better not let it affect me. So they opened the door, and there's this old woman stretched out, naked as a jaybird, on the prep table. The embalming was in progress. They were pumping the arterial fluid in and the color was just about coming back—sort of a pale pink color. There was something very artificial about it. You know the old line when you go to a funeral and the relatives file by the casket and take a last glimpse of what's-his-name, and somebody says, "Gee, he looks so natural"—ridiculous! Anyway, all of my preconceived ideas of what was on the other side of the door were really unfounded.

You know there are so many old wives' tales about dead people: their skin is clammy and rubbery, they all turn blue, all these kinds of things. What I discovered seeing my first dead body—you know, not dressed or laid out in a coffin— was just that . . . hey, there's nothing there, just a shell. It was like a naked dummy in a store window. I was surprised that it wasn't something more. It's almost like that song Peggy Lee sings, "Is That All There Is?" I was saying to myself, is that all there is to death?

I worked afternoons and Saturdays. My duties varied from dusting furniture to washing the cars. I think they sensed that I was treating this as if it were any other job. They realized it didn't bother me, so little by little they let me do more things. Legally I couldn't do any embalming, but I could help dress bodies and lay them out. Afterwards I would clean up; you know, do the old Ajax routine on the prep table to get off the dried blood and everything else. That part didn't bother me either. There was this one guy I worked with, Pete, who was also going to school and worked there part-time. He was a typical college student in the mid- to late sixties. He would always come in stoned; you know, he'd have a joint or so before coming to work just to get his head on straight. I think that is probably the only way he could take it. He didn't like going into the prep room, it made him queasy. He never really got into it . . . not that you're supposed to.

                         *   *   *

I became calloused toward it; maybe systemized is a better word for it. It becomes routine. I can recite verbatim what's gonna happen when somebody dies: the coach is sent out to pick up the body; they're brought in, taken off the stretcher, and put into the prep room. Then they're embalmed, and afterwards comes the cosmetology. Then they're laid out in the casket . . . and the show begins—only the actors are different; the plot's always the same.

It can get real hectic at times. I mean, when it rains it really does pour. We've had as many as four, sometimes five, going on; you know, it'll be real slow and then it all happens at once. It can get pretty comical. Now you start playing musical bodies and hope like hell you don't misplace anybody, you don't get Mrs. Jones in the Mrs. Smith funeral.

You've got only one two-table prep room, so you're gassing two of 'em up. You've got the other two lined up in the hallway. You finish one and the hairdresser's got to come in, so you wheel 'im into the chapel area where there's room to work. Sometimes you feel like a traffic cop in the Lincoln Tunnel; you know, you're pushing bodies, pushing bodies. Then all of a sudden you get a call: there's been a car accident and you've got to take two people out to the morgue and pick 'em up. So that leaves only one guy back in the prep room working very feverishly—sort of like a butcher might work in a wholesale meat market trying to get things squared away before the next truckload comes in.

I guess I have become calloused to the whole thing, so much so that I can go to the funeral of a friend and it's very hard for me to feel remorse or grief. I don't look at the body, because to me it's just a show. Maybe that sounds cruel, but that's the attitude that I've developed from working within the industry.

When I go to a funeral, the first thing I start looking at is the home, the condition of it. I like to see how the flowers are laid out. Recently at one funeral that I attended, I noticed that the tables and lamps were dusty. So on the way out—the funeral director was at the door shaking everybody's hands and saying goodbye and thank you—I shook his hand and said, "I think you ought to dust the lamps and tables." He went, "Huh?" It freaked him out. Then I told him, "Hey, I worked in a funeral home too."

I think my work made me kinda lackadaisical about death. One day Bert got a call that a fellow who lived up the street from him died, fellow by the name of Horace Whitby. So Bert says, "C'mon, let's go down and pick up Horace." So we got in the coach and drove down. We pulled up in Horace's driveway and took the stretcher out of the back. Horace's wife was waiting for us at the door. She let us in, we wheeled the stretcher down the hall and into the bedroom, and there's Horace in bed, still in his pajamas. I guess this was around noon. He had slept a little bit on the late side that morning. His wife had given him a big breakfast, maybe three hours ago, and he died—just like that.

So we pulled back the bed sheets and Bert says, "Okay, what do you want, the head or the feet?" So we lifted him out of the bed—no problem, right? Except when we picked him up, he sort of sagged in the rear and passed all kinds of wind . . . not even realizing it because he was dead. I looked at Bert and his face was red. I figured Bert must have farted, but I didn't say anything 'cause Horace's wife was right there. So we rolled Horace out of there and put him into the coach. As we drove off, I turned to Bert and said, "Boy, you let out a hell of a fart back there." He says, "Whaduhya mean me? That was Horace. That was his goodbye to the world." That was his concept of death, I guess.

*   *   *

A lot of my friends, when they found out I was working in a funeral home, would ask, "How do you look sad?" I used to answer them quite frankly, that it's hard to look sad at a funeral when you're getting paid. For the most part, you didn't know the people, so it was sort of easy not to be emotionally involved and to be detached from the situation. An air, a look of dignity has to be established; people sort of expect you to show outward signs of remorse. It's a face you put on, it's a role; and I had to play the role that I thought people would expect. You know, the typical attendant, standing there very straight, solemn; black suit, black tie, hair neatly combed. Not grievous looking, but expressing some concern; shaking their hands with a "how do you do" in a very low tone, sort of a looking-at-the-floor type of manner. You wouldn't want to see a guy in cut-off blue jeans with long freaky hair and a beard handing out a memory booklet at your Uncle Charlie's funeral.

Funeral directors are very conscious about their public image. Again, it's role playing. When they're being paid that kind of money, how the hell do you look sad? Really, how can you? I don't mean that they're going to be exuberant or joyful, you know, "Hey, this is a $6,000 funeral, wow!" But they can't get emotionally involved either, it would be destroying. After all is said and done, you don't keep on the black suit and somber expression. Funeral directors are human like any one of us, and they have their moments when they just have to let off steam and be human again. They go to conventions and get loaded and have a good time just like everybody else.

*   *   *

People say, how could anybody do that kind of work. Somebody's got to do it. Like the guy who collects your garbage, if he's a good garbage collector, he has pride in his work and he has a feeling of worth. With a funeral director, it's the same thing. I really didn't mean to make that analogy—maybe it was a Freudian slip or something, I don't know—but it's not an easy job and there is a certain amount of reverence, respect and pride that goes along with it.

People are always dumping on funeral directors; you know, they take advantage of people at a time when they're really not able to think logically or realistically. Nobody plans to die. We all know it's gonna happen, but we never plan for it. Who would write down, I'd like to be buried in a solid walnut casket with a blue felt lining? Nobody does.

I had great regard and esteem for the funeral directors I worked for. They were genuinely concerned with helping families get through this difficult time. They would take a family back into the casket display room and show them the different styles and models—from a $250 cloth-covered casket to a $5,000 solid cherry or mahogany—and stand in the background and let them make their own choices.

It comes down to professional ethics. Any funeral director worth his salt will not sell a family. It's the same with a car salesman. On one side of the coin, you have the guy who is honestly concerned; he doesn't want to oversell you. He wants to sell you something you're going to be happy with, because he is looking at you down the road. If he gives you good service, you won't feel you're being ripped off and you'll come back to him. On the other side of the coin, there is the guy that believes in the old used car adage: there's an ass for every seat. I'm sure the same thing holds true for the funeral industry.

It's not so much funeral directors who are screwed up, it's the people—the survivors, the family—that mess it up. As an attendant, you are the low man on the totem pole. You don't deal directly with the family, but maybe you're polishing the furniture or vacuuming the carpet while the family is in making the arrangements, and you overhear what's going on.

Okay, Uncle Charlie dies, and his son, Ralph, and daughter, Bessie, come in to make the arrangements. Now, let's say they come from a prominent family. There is a certain amount of prestige in how one handles a funeral, and they want to keep up the airs. They are now in charge of impressing everyone. It's like going out and buying a Cadillac. Now, the funeral director is sitting behind his desk trying to keep a straight face and thinking to himself, what a couple of silly asses.

"I think Dad would have wanted a nice solid cherry casket."

"Golly, he would love to have a copper-lined vault."

"Gee, he didn't have a plot, so we'll get him a special one at such-and-such cemetery."

Now, all the trappings are thrown in on top of that. Maybe the guy was a bum in real life, he may have been a heel, but they are thinking in terms of the prestige of the family: how will this reflect on me.

Maybe they are trying to satisfy their own feelings of guilt. They feel that this is sort of making up for how they treated this person in life. It's a hell of a time to show it, after the fact. It's the same with friends. Let's say you and Charlie were "old buddies." Maybe you haven't seen the guy in twenty years, but you're "sorry to see him go." So, as the result of guilt or prestige, you get the florist on the phone:

"Old Charlie was a great guy, I want something nice for him. Now, make sure you sign it 'Garrett Hartmann.' Put it in big letters, 'My sincerest condolences, GARRETT, that's with two r's and two t's, HARTMANN, that's H-a-r-t-m-a-double-n.' "

It's funny how death sort of reunites families. By some almost mystical power they're drawn together. You didn't think enough of Uncle Charlie to send him a Christmas card last year, you probably forgot his birthday, you didn't send him a get-well card, but you show up at the funeral. Whammo!, all of a sudden, the relatives pour in from out of town. They probably haven't seen each other for ten years—you know, since the last funeral. "The last time I saw you was at Aunt Tessie's wake." Then comes the old line, "It's a shame that we have to meet under circumstances like these."

You know the old story: you can't please all the people all the time. The minute you get more than three people at a funeral, you're going to have somebody that's going to object to something. It's the funeral director's job to try to maintain his cool, his *savoir faire,* even though the family all around him is going bullshit. The funeral director is trying to be Mr. Impartial in a field of feuding relatives.

Now, the position of the flowers is very important. The floral pieces from the immediate family have to be prominently displayed in front of the casket. The other pieces are arranged according to prestige. You try to get a balanced arrangement—yellow mums with yellow buttons, and so on. You try to give the whole thing an artistic semblance.

The first thing when somebody comes in to view the body, there's a quick glance over. Usually for the women it's a little more emotional, but for the men it's, you know, "Oh, gee, there he is." Then they go immediately to the flowers and start reading all the cards. They're not reading the cards to find out who sent all the flowers, but to find out where theirs are. Then they'll come over to the funeral director and say, "Hey, I don't want my bouquet over here, I want it moved over there." Or someone would sort of get me aside: "See my bouquet there over on the floor? Couldn't you get it a little closer to Charlie? Look, see that one over there? Now, that one's from Aunt Matilda; now, she wasn't very close to him, she's been out in California for the past thirty years. Why don't you just switch ours?"

There is a certain amount of ceremony, rigamarole that goes on. Of course, the person's mourned for a time, and then, bing!, the service is over at the grave site, and as they file past him you hear the little murmurs:

'He never liked that church anyway."

"Why'd they have to put him here? I wouldn't have put him here."

"You know, that was Ralph's fault. He was handling all of the arrangements."

"Well, certainly if they gave *me* the opportunity, I wouldn't have set it up this way."

Then the bickering goes on. You overhear little tidbits:

"Gee, I wonder who'll get the antique vase. You know the one. Gosh, I had my eye on that for years. I hope she doesn't get in there and get it before I do. You know, she's back from California, and she's just liable to go over there and go over the whole place before we get a chance."

"Well, now that he's dead, I s'pose Ralph'll take all the money and we won't see a penny of it."

It sounds like a Vegas comedy routine, but it really happens. The hardest part when you hear it is to keep a straight face, because inside you're laughing like hell and you say to yourself, My God, don't these people know any better. Those dumb bastards, this is not the way it's supposed to be. What's the matter with you, the guy's in the ground five minutes and you're worried what your share is going to be. You see what goes on, you see the sham that's being made out of a person's funeral, and you can't help but say to yourself, geez, I hope like hell that never happens to me.

*   *   *

We just had a little informal class reunion of high school kids the other day. It came up in conversation that I worked for a funeral home when I was in college. Everybody turned around and looked at me and said, "What? What did you do? Did you touch 'em? No, you didn't do that, did you? What's it like?" The curiosity about death—what's it like. None of us has ever seen the other side of that big dark wall. Once you step through it, you can't spread apart a

tiny hole and yell back, "Hey, it's not bad," or, "Get me out
of here." I can remember when I was a child, laying in bed
thinking what it would be like when I'm dead; Not being
able to see my family or look out at the trees and grass, or
play with my dog. I still don't have any answers in terms
of death. I only worked with it.

I can't conceive of God creating life and then having it
all end in a split second. Obviously, as one person dies,
hundreds are born. Someone may come along to pick up
what you started or may tear down everything that you
built . . . but there's gotta be something after. As to what
it's like, I don't know; none of us do. I don't buy this bit
about harps and clouds, nor do I buy the concept of hell
either. Your life here can be your heaven or hell, depending
on what you want to make it. Still and all, regardless of
whether you believe in a great glorious hereafter or an
inferno, it all boils down to the fact that we gotta live
with each other the best we can.

When you're young, you don't like to think about death.
Like those insurance commercials: life insurance?—I don't
want to talk about it! I guess human beings like to think
that it always happens to the other guy. We never really
expect it's going to happen to us. After my experience with
funerals, I think I'm more aware of death and have more
reverence for life. You see what goes on, you see the sham,
and you have a better awareness of what life is supposed
to be all about.

It's funny—not funny, ha-ha, but funny, tragic. There was
an old woman who lived across the street from us. I guess
about a year ago she was put into a home. Well, she died
about three weeks ago and my wife and I went to her
funeral. We were down at the cemetery and they were putting down the artificial grass, getting ready for the count-
down, for the lowering into the big deep abyss in the
ground, covered with plastic flowers. Her son walked up to
us and I said, "I'm sorry about your mother." And he says,

"Why? You know it was the damnedest thing about that old broad. For years she lived at home and was fine, then I put her in a home for 300 bucks a week, and she falls, breaks her hip and dies."

I guess I sort of ended up with the philosophy of life that I would do whatever I could to try and live life to the fullest and try to be a better human being while I'm still here. Why be a miserable son of a bitch, when with a little bt of finesse you can be loved. Why have them say over your casket, "Thank God that rotten old bastard's gone."

In Memoriam

Julia Chen, forty, is a painter and a sculptor.

I have studied many times
The marble which was chiseled for me—
A boat with a furled sail at rest in a harbor.
In truth it pictures not my destination
But my life.
For love was offered me and I shrank from its disillusionment;
Sorrow knocked at my door, but I was afraid;
Ambition called to me, but I dreaded the chances.
Yet all the while I hungered for meaning in my life.
And now I know that we must lift the sail
And catch the winds of destiny
Wherever they drive the boat.
To put meaning in one's life may end in madness,
But life without meaning is the torture
Of restlessness and vague desire—
It is a boat longing for the sea and yet afraid.
                                        —Edgar Lee Masters

I'm not a mystical person at all, but these things have come
to me through visions. I would wake up in the night and
have visions of bodies in containers. Most of my visions
have been architectural, a structure with a body inside. The
first piece which I finished was a sarcophagus. I saw it in a
direct vision and knew that I had to make it.

I became very interested in Egyptology. I started to plan
my own funeral in the Egyptian style. It was a very auto-

biographical funeral; I wanted to tell my life. I wanted the
art that would survive me to be a statement: this is who
I was.

I've lost that impetus now. I no longer have it, though
I made my own shroud. My shroud is a kind of philosoph·
ical plaything. Death is not a reality to me. I still cannot
focus on the idea that I will cease to be. By associating
myself with things connected with death and the funeral,
I am trying to work out my own death terror.

To me, this is nitty-gritty art. I don't feel that I'm any
more obsessed with my subject than Cézanne was obsessed
with fruits on a table. My work is about the urge towards
immortality. I don't know, but I don't think there is any
afterlife. It has no basis in reality. But we have the urge,
therefore we must act upon it. I want to live forever; I want
the people I love to live forever. I don't believe that it can
happen, but of course I hope. If there is any magic I can
perform, I'm going to try.

I don't think my work is going to make me as a person
immortal. As far as people remembering me as a person, I
know that is futility. I have no hopes of that whatsoever.
I think people have too many things to do with their lives
to remember. I don't think of Shakespeare or Mozart as
people, as living flesh and blood—they are words or notes
on a page. I only hope that my work survives.

*   *   *

My life has always been associated with death. When I
was three years old, my grandfather died while I was in his
arms. When my other grandfather died a few years later, I
remember my father's attitude towards my mother's grieving: "Stop your crying, Lillian. I don't want to hear it.
Everybody dies—you're going to die, I'm doing to die, your
children are going to die."

I had a pet chicken, a bantam rooster that he let me have.

I remember picking him out; they came a hundred chickens to the box. One day a few months later, when I came home from school, my father told me, "You have to kill your chicken." He took me to the woodshed and he gave me his ax. I was a small child, maybe eight years old. I had this huge ax in my hand; I was crying. He didn't want me to cry; he kept slapping me. He said, "You must not get attached to things. Don't love, it's better not to love, it's too painful." But I did love the chicken, and I killed the chicken.

This is the theme that ran through my childhood, this love and death thing. This uncertainty, this insecurity. I began to hate my father and wanted to kill him. He was a cruel man and had a very cruel laugh. I hated my mother because she did not protect me.

I have been married three times and had many affairs; friendships with women don't last. I have to keep pushing people away. I can see what I used to call my nihilism is a reflection of my own experience. I was taught that life was basically hopeless. You're never going to get what you want. Do not try to get close to people because they will only disappoint you, hurt you, desert you, and die.

In a sense, the subject matter of my work reflects that pain, that hopelessness. I think that is one reason why I selected it. It is an important issue—I guess it's *the* issue of life.

I think the stability of death, the unchangeability, has an appeal to me. When I think of my childhood, there was this contrast and ambiguity between the maniacal atmosphere I lived in and the beauty of the countryside. A part of my personal solution to pain is to cover it over with beauty.

*   *   *

One thing I'm trying to say with my work is: care for the dead. Our feelings do not stop just because a person is dead. You've cared for these people; lavish some attention on them. Give them beauty. Give yourself a chance to grieve. I'm not talking about spending a lot of money on the dead. Making out a check for $5,000 is a hell of a lot different than helping your mother select her shroud.

I think the way we treat the dead is a very good barometer as to how we treat the living. I think when funerals are meaningless, cold and sterile, our society is meaningless, cold and sterile. Convention is very often a shorthand for feelings. It's very unimaginative. You really don't have to become involved: Oh, this is what we do now, we order flowers.

I see this as part of a much larger issue. It is part of the grand scheme of oppression. It works to the political advantage of people who are against freedom. As the funeral industry, the hospital industry, all industries, play a greater role in our lives, it is expedient to have people who don't feel or think. They are much easier to manipulate than people who do feel or think . . . In a sense, there are other ways of dying than dying.

Elegy in a Country Churchyard

Frank D'Angelo, fifty-five, is a gravedigger.

You might say I was kind of born into this job. My dad was superintendent of another cemetery for over twenty-five years. I've been diggin' graves by hand since I was six years old—as soon as I could hold a shovel I started diggin' graves. I never had no schoolin'. Anybody with book learnin' is a wiz over me, but when it comes to practical knowledge he's up a creek without a paddle. I had a couple of heart attacks six years ago, and I'm still workin' like heck.

You see a lot of things workin' in a cemetery over the years, and it's somethin' to glory over and somethin' to laugh over. I can remember a time back in '36 or '37—I was only a young pup. There was this guy who used to own a candy store. He kicked me in the behind one time—you know, maybe he caught me stealin' a piece of candy or makin' too much noise or somethin'. I says, "I'll get you when you die, you bastard" . . . so a couple of years after that the guy died. I spit right on his grave.

In the winter months you gotta go like hell to dig a grave. I've seen the frost as high as thirty-eight inches. You go nuts. You dig a grave and the pile of dirt freezes on you, so we used to get a pick and maybe a sledge hammer and a chisel to chop up these chunks of dirt. We would throw in these big chunks of dirt just to fill this hole—the quicker we got this hole filled the quicker we went home.

One time, a good many years ago, it was around Easter
time and the ground started to warm up, and with this hot
sun comin' up this lady, Mrs. Santucci, was over there
prayin' by her husband's grave. All of a sudden this grave
takes a drop; I'd say about two feet. Them big chunks must
have thawed out or somethin'. The dirt just literally caved
right into the grave and the lady is hollerin' in I-talian that
her husband is trying to grab her and pull her in the grave.
We cracked up—we died laughin'.

Over the years we had three or four suicides. One time
this young fella—I'd say he was about thirty-five—he had this
girlfriend. I used to see him every once in a while put a
flower on her grave. One day I happened to walk over in
this area and I seen somethin' was wrong. So I quick ran; I
had to run a half mile to the nearest phone. I called a priest,
then the police. When they came down they found this guy
sprawled out on this grave, pills all over.

Another time, it was in the mornin' and I had to dig a
grave for a funeral comin' in. It was kinda chilly, so when
I was done, the vaultman and I went out for coffee. We
came back and were standin' up facin' the sun tryin' to get
a little warm, and I see a car way up in the corner. I says,
"Jeezus, how long has that car been there?" The windows
were all steamed up. I says, "Uh-oh, we must have lovers;
let's check 'em out. Listen, I'll sneak around and if anybody is gettin' fixed up I'll give you the high sign and you
come over; we'll watch 'em and *then* chase 'em."

Well, when I walked up towards the car I seen somethin'
wasn't right. I quick ran down to the phone and called the
priest. I says, "Father, somebody had a heart attack in here."
Then I notified the police. When I got back I seen somethin' different. There was a hose attached to the exhaust
pipe of the car runnin' into the back window. He had one
of these dogs with him that's always on the fire trucks—
Dalmatians. My God, when the police got there and opened
the door the car was still runnin'. He had a half a tank of

gas left. That man was deader than a doornail along with the dog. Now, we had a funeral comin' in at 10:15, and here we got seven police cars, an ambulance, all them red lights flashin', and doggone it all them people are wonderin' what the hell is goin' on and nobody's concerned with the funeral.

*   *   *

The biggest problem down here are these people that are ten-cent millionaires. They want everything done right away and hurry up, and then you never see them again—they don't even come down to put a Christmas decoration on, unless maybe the day after Christmas and then they get it for nothin'. On the other hand, you got these poor old devils that are on Social Security, don't know where the next meal's comin' from, and they'll give you a dollar tip.

A while back—it was on a holiday—everybody was off except me and the old gent who works with me. We had to carry this casket over a hundred yards, and this funeral director hands me two dollars—*on a holiday*. I says to him, "Can you spare this?" I gave it to the old gent 'cause he don't make too much money, and I walked away. A week later the lady whose husband I buried comes up—I've known her for years. The first thing I said to her was, where in the hell did you get the cheap goddamned undertaker. I told her what happened and she said, "My God, I paid for pallbearers, why did you have to carry the casket?" I said, "Well, there was no pallbearers here," and she says, "Well, I just got the bill from the funeral director and you should see the amount of money he's got marked down for tips." I said, "The cemetery only got two dollars, you call him up and ask him to send you an itemized slip of the tips, where they went." Now what did this undertaker do with the tips? You know, people always ask me if I see ghosts and this and that. I always have a good answer for 'em. I don't worry about ghosts. The only thing I've got to worry about is the living—they're the ones that rob you.

*   *   *

Years gone back it used to be very emotional. People would throw themselves on the casket, and when they stood there and watched the coffin go into the hole—forget about it, it took them an hour before they left, the way they carried on. Today they are kinda gettin' away from that. Once in a while we still get families and have this carryin' on, but the people are hypocrites. They carry on at the cemetery like heck, but why didn't they take care of the person when he was alive? They didn't do it . . . yet when they come to the cemetery, they carry on blue-murder.

When I die, I want to be cremated. I figure most of the people don't come back to the cemetery and visit anyhow, so what's the sense of having a guy in the ground and nobody's even gonna come and put a rose on 'im.

All the talk you hear about life after death—I don't believe it . . . Na, you're gone, that's it. When my Dad died, two weeks later my youngest son was born. Maybe that's got something to do with it. There may be somethin' to it . . . but I doubt it.

I'll tell you right now, after a couple of heart attacks, I'm scared. I don't want to die. Life is too nice, and you're dead for a helluva long time.

Elysian Fields

Fred Phillips, forty-three, is the manager of a privately owned cemetery.

I don't have a "thing" about death like most people do. It's just a chemical reaction—you're done. I can't conceive of an afterlife, I just can't. You live only once. That doesn't mean you live chaotically; you can't have anarchy. I'm not anti-religion, I'm just not religious. Anything man can't explain, he puts a different definition on. Like the early Stone Age men would attribute lightning and thunder to gods because they couldn't explain it.

Look at the average age of your church attendants; see those who take up the faith once more. I just think it's a typical example of man's hedging by taking out insurance. It's the only way man can face old age and face dying . . . the fear of the unknown. (My father's a living example of this, and I wish he'd get off my back.) The closer you get, the more you pay the higher premiums on your "insurance policy."

People go to great lengths to duck death in any way, shape or form. They can enjoy it on the television, or in any vicarious situation—but boy, don't bring it to their own yard; they don't want to know. There are some people who will not buy graves because they feel it's like condemning themselves. There was a very nice, intelligent gentleman in his forties who bought some graves here. His friends said he shouldn't have done it because he was jinxing himself. Of course, we all laughed at that. He called us up twenty-

four hours later and told us to open one. His twenty-year-old
son was hit by a train. Now that wasn't too cool; here we
were laughing at the irony of jinxing yourself, and twenty-
four hours later there was a tragedy. But that was just a
random shot, a coincidence.

One thing you see in the cemetery is the conscience
offerings of people. We have a lady here who is a fanatic
about her husband's grave. She is on our "pest" list at this
point—she can really nag and be a pest; she is completely
unreasonable. For six months she has been in every day.
Call it amateur psychology or what, but we happen to feel
that maybe she had something to do with this gentleman
being put in early.

People ask me, does it ever get to you working on this
job. The idea of working with death doesn't mean a thing
to me. Actually the death part of this job is really . . . five
percent. The rest is maintenance. Once, a little girl died
and was buried here. Her mother was in hysterics. The girl
was the same age as one of my daughters, and the vulnerability of how I would feel if it were one of my daughters
got to me. Otherwise . . . I had one day when I had three
or four weepy ones right in a row. They want to tell you
the story of their life. I just will not get involved; I will not
sympathize. I am cold—polite, but cold: Yes, yes, that's interesting, and change the subject. I don't want to be too cold,
I don't want to give them the cold shoulder, I just won't get
with them.

I just turn it off . . . detached is a better word for it. How
does a doctor handle it? How does a nurse survive when
somebody on the floor dies? You just don't get involved.
Of course, they are all wonderful people, everybody is a
wonderful person somewhere along the line, but . . . we
bury boxes, that's it.

The only time it becomes people . . . getting back to
man's almighty drive—I'm burying a person as opposed to
a box this Friday. That person's family was worth a few

hundred dollars in commissions to me . . . that's not bad
for an hour's work. Now, I'm on salary and my commission
is ten percent. So what's ten percent of a big grave sale:
the most expensive grave is $375.50, my commission is
$37.50. Okay, it's nice, but you're not going to write home
about it. But when someone comes in and buys a half dozen
graves or so in the top line . . . ah. . . .

5

On Immortality

Heaven but the vision of fulfilled desire,
And hell the shadow from a soul on fire,
Cast on the darkness into which ourselves,
So late emerged from, shall so soon expire.

—Omar Khayyam;
translated by E. Fitzgerald.

The Other Side

Joe Fiorello, eighty-one, worked as a gardener on a large private estate for close to fifty years. He is a widower and lives with his youngest son.

I enjoyed my life and I enjoyed my work. All my life I make things grow. Now you take when I use to work—I walk one hour every morning and one hour every night. Now, you jam on the car, five-a minutes you over there. People today they no stand still like they use to. They go up and down, up and down. The world—it go up and down.

Money ain't everything. If I had good my eyes, if I had my leg good; if I could go to work again, I go to work. Now, you take the boss I use to work. He had all the money in the world—he told me lots of times. One day he called me—he use to call me Joe-boy. "Joe-boy," he says, "I got all the money in the world, but money ain't everything. You got to have good health." He was in the city the next morning. He called his wife and after ten minutes he drop dead.

I don't know about the future. You can't tell. Maybe I go sleep and not get up in the morning. It is the only way I like to go. You no suffer anymore. I hope if I done a good thing, I get a good thing on the other side. I hope it's better than this place—better than over here. I don't know . . . nobody knows. I think probably I go plant tomatoes on the other side.

Visions of Heaven and Hell

Epathrus, twenty-two, and Levi, seventeen, are followers of The Children of God, a religious cult founded in California in the late sixties.

LEVI: I never worried about myself dying. I had a lot of ideas about pre-destiny; you know, things were just going to happen no matter what. I guess I had a pretty fatalistic attitude about everything. I never thought I was a very good person. I was brought up going to church and stuff, and there they seemed to come on with the idea that if you're not good you're gonna go to hell. So I thought, well, one of these days I'm gonna go to hell; you know, I thought, well, I've got plenty of time . . .

EPATHRUS: Both of us used to take drugs and stuff like that. I didn't know where I was going. I didn't know that I was bad. I did have a fear about death, but when I received Jesus into my heart . . . well like right now, I might be afraid of the pain of death, but of actually dying, I'm not afraid.

LEVI: It's not something I really look forward to. Like right now I'm seventeen; I don't know what it's like to be twenty or twenty-five; I don't know what's gonna happen tomorrow. I guess it would be fine with me to die of old age. It would be interesting to live through all the stages of life; but if I was told I only had a short time to live, I wouldn't worry about it. I think it will be a nice experience

144

when it comes. I'd probably be kinda excited, but then again I'd feel sorry for the people like my family and friends who wouldn't understand the way I feel. You know, they'd say it's terrible and that would make me feel bad.

I would feel sad in a way to leave my family and friends, but more joy in that I would be with Jesus and other brothers and sisters from past ages whom I've never met. Like when I left home to serve God, I left my family and a lot of friends. I really love my parents more than I ever did before, and every now and then I go to visit them. I still do feel the desire to be with my friends, but you have to decide what is more important to you; it all comes down to what is more important. Like when I die, I think it would be terrible for someone to cry over me because I'm dead and especially to come and look at my physical body. The physical part of it is really irrelevant.

EPATHRUS: You know, it's just a body. You did live in it, but so what; a building with nobody livin' in it is just dead brick. The only things that you can keep are just good memories; those are the things that are important.

LEVI: This tradition of paying last respects I think gets carried away and everything gets real mechanical. I don't know, I've always rebelled against traditions and stuff, but that's what it seems like to me.

EPATHRUS: You know, society really puts a lot of emphasis on physical, outward show but really neglects the inner spiritual thing. I think that's really hypocritical and it's really sad too. Like parents take really good care of their children in a material sense, but neglect to give them the time, love and understanding they need.

I guess I'd want some kind of funeral, but I wouldn't want a great big thing. Some people feel, well it's my last thing, I might as well make it a big deal. It's become more of a money-making deal. You know. Like someone's just died; people are feeling sorry, they should have spent more time with the person. A funeral director comes in . . . Okay, he does a job, but he can overdo it too—you know, play it up. I can't see spending a few thousand dollars on a casket for someone who has just died. I wouldn't want that money spent on me; I'd want it spent on something that's living. It just seems kind of silly. There is nothing wrong with spending some time with the family and thinking about the person, but to spend lots of money, and the way that kind of thing is done . . . I think it's kinda bad. It's like a put-on.

In the Bible this one guy said he was gonna follow Jesus but first he had to bury his father. Jesus said to the guy, "Let the dead bury the dead"; in other words, let them get into it, the people who are really into it, but you come and follow me; follow the living and let's get on with life.

I remember one guy—this kinda stuck in my mind—he said, "You know, when I die I don't want to have a big funeral, dark clothes and stuff like that; what I want to have is a parade. I want to go down the street and have a couple of guys playing music; in a way kinda happy, but sad. You know, people kinda remembering the good times you had together rather than everyone wearing black, that kind of thing, not in a sober, terrible way." It shouldn't be a bad thing; it's something we should accept because it's part of life, and it's something that's gonna happen to everybody.

LEVI: For myself, they can just dig a hole and throw me in. Then all my brothers and sisters will probably say, "I wish I could have gone with him."

EPATHRUS: It won't be floating around on pink clouds and banging on a harp. That would be a drag. It's gonna be far-out. It'll be exciting, full of sights and sounds—all sorts of things.

LEVI: I think that there'll be some small villages where everyone is just farming the land.

EPATHRUS: You know, getting back to all those kinds of basic natural things—living off the land, sharing, loving and working together.

LEVI: There will be an absence of negative thought within you. It will be like you're always happy.

EPATHRUS: I think hell would be like people just totally frustrated with what they are doing, working all their lives and never getting anywhere; doing the same thing over and over again, life just goes on and on and on. Hell might just be a continuation of what's happening on earth right now.

From what I can understand, I figure we're livin' really close to the end. Just take a look around; it's really a big mess. I consider a place like New York City to be just about like hell.

LEVI: Yeah, that's really heavy.

Nobody's Ever Come Back
and Complained

Dominick Falcone, sixty-two, has been a funeral director for more than forty years.

The average man who does not know what to do with his life, wants another one which will last forever.
— Anatole France

There isn't going to be any more death, so I guess I'd be out of business. As far as money is concerned, there is no problem up there; they don't use it. If you have to work, well, I think your work should be what is necessary for that type of living. I guess somebody will tell me . . . you know, make suggestions for what I should do.

I don't know if you actually go right to God or not, but I do believe in God enough to think that I'm going to be with him someday. I visualize it as being a very pleasant atmosphere; people are all pleasant, no sinners around. You meet your family that's gone before you. Everybody loves everybody; every race, color or creed, everybody's happy.

They'll do everything together—sing, play baseball, play golf. The same baseball player down here will probably be hitting the ball up there. Maybe up there I'd be able to break par. It can't be all that bad.

Like my mother-in-law always says, nobody's ever come back and complained.

This Has Got to Be Hell

Chuck McKenzie, thirty-four, is an emergency medical technician and a fireman.

When I first came on the job, I started keeping count of the DOA's. After two or three months, I lost count. Now I couldn't say how many. There's lots of people dying. You feel bad about it, but dying is the same as living. A certain amount of people have to die and a certain amount of people have to be born.

I'm sort of a sentimental guy . . . I cry and get choked up at good tear-jerkers on TV. But in this job, if I was emotional, I couldn't work on anybody. You try not to get personally involved because it could destroy you. Sometimes you start questioning yourself: Did I perform right, did I do the right thing, were my decisions right. But usually once I get a person to the hospital, that's it, they're wiped clean from my mind.

A lot of times we get bitter at the hospital. Here we got a person saved and a few minutes later he dies in the emergency room. We'll say, "Hey, they killed another one." When they were adding to the hospital to make the emergency room larger, we said they should have made the morgue bigger instead. We're not actually blaming them, but we sort of put it on them to keep it off ourselves.

I've had people throwing up clots of blood like bowls of Jell-O, and I'll come back and finish my dinner. We had one man who was dead for five or six days. It was in extreme heat and all the windows were closed in his apartment. Man, if you want to talk about stench, we had to put the breathing apparatus on to go in. When we rolled his body over, there were billions and billions of maggots crawling in and out. It was unreal, but I was able to handle it. We even managed to joke about it. As we were driving him to the morgue, my partner goes to me, "Hey Chuck, take a look and see if that guy is crawling around back there." You know, you gotta keep your wits about you. I felt creepy and crawly all night. That's one night I didn't eat.

I can handle this job; I can handle people dying in the worst ways possible, but when it comes to kids . . . I had a little boy who was hit by a car. The car rolled over him and he was pinned underneath. The whole front of his body was burnt from being dragged on the ground. You gotta handle this. I was able to do what emergency medical treatment had to be done, but once I got him into the ambulance, I had to calm myself down as well as calming him and his mother down. My throat was so swelled up I couldn't talk at first.

A few weeks ago we had two little kids run over by a car and killed. They were walking on the sidewalk with their mother and this woman came down a one-way street the wrong way. Not only was she half in the bag, but she was running away from another accident that she'd just had. She lost control of her car and ran over these two little kids. Man, let me tell you, I thank God I wasn't working that day. I don't know how I would have handled it. The guy who rode on that, he's got a couple of small kids. It still bothers him.

*   *   *

People who attempt suicide make me angry. Life is good. You should hang in there, seek help if you have a problem, but don't try and take your life. I had a young girl who overdosed on Sleep-Eze, Contac, Excedrin, and a giant bottle of wine. She got scared and called her boyfriend. Most people who call somebody don't want to die, they want attention. They ain't gonna get it from me. I'm not gonna be treatin' 'em nice, soft-soapin' 'em; I'm gonna treat 'em as rough as I can. You have to show 'em that what they done is wrong. I told this girl, "You just wanted attention; well, you ain't gonna get it from me. When we get to the hospital, they're gonna pump ya."

Sometimes when we get to the hospital we assist the staff. I held this girl down as they were shoving the tube down her throat. I said to her, "Was it worth what you did? Would you do it again? Well, I sure as hell hope you learned your goddamn lesson." Maybe I'm pushing my beliefs and my upbringing onto this person. I know it's not up to me to say who's to live and who's to die, but I'm gonna try to do what I can to make sure that they do try to live.

*   *   *

I'm not overly religious; I don't go to church every Sunday. I can't remember the last time I went to church, but I believe that I'm gonna go to heaven when I die—you gotta go to heaven, because our life here on earth is nothing but hurts, hardships, hospitalizations; one disaster after another. Of course you have your happy times, but you're paying for your sins now. I believe we're living in hell. Boy, I'll tell ya, this has got to be hell. It has to be.

The Skeptic

Mary Janczyk, fifty-eight, is a part-time sales clerk.

My Father Christmas passed away
When I was barely seven
At twenty-one, alack-a-day,
I lost my hope of heaven.

Yet not in either lies the curse:
The hell of it's because
I don't know which loss hurt the worse—
My God or Santa Claus.
                                    —Robert Service

You hear and read in the paper about people who have almost died, and how they say how beautiful it is. Well . . . it's something to think about, but on the other hand, there is nothing they can tell us about after death. We all can theorize about it and imagine what is going to happen, but nobody really knows.

I think, if you are supposed to meet people up there . . . how's this possible? Eternity—it would take an eternity to find anybody. So, I'm very skeptical about how it would be possible.

Most people think about going to heaven and all this. I think most people like to feel that way. I do myself . . . and yet I can't convince myself that this is so, that we all will be floating around someplace.

Love and Death

Sister Mary Bonaventure, seventy, is an elementary school teacher.

But when I pass from death into life,
I already know I'll agree with you, Lord.
And this sea of days
will be as a speck in my memory.
Then I shall understand
how beautiful were the psalms at evening;
and the dew that unseen you scattered
on meadows with delicate hands at night.
I shall remember the lichen
that one day you spread
over the crumbling wall of the convent:
then I shall see it as a gigantic tree
covering the ruins. Then I shall hear again
the sweetness of morning bells
that awakened such melancholy in me
at every encounter with the light.
Then I shall know with what patience
you waited for me; and with what love
you prepared me for marriage.
And death refused to take me.
I wept from my loneliness
but you fed on it.
Never did my heart intone a song of joy,
dazed by the fragrance of things created.
Every voice of love was a sob. Instead
it was You I smelled in my flesh,
You hidden in every desire,
O infinite, who weighed on my embraces.
The same quiver, or storm, on the surface
of the sea as within the waves of the chalice.

*You were everywhere. And while the kisses of others
stopped at the mouth,
I ate You at every dawn.
And why then, why then
was I so sad?*

—David Maria Turoldo

We all aim for happiness. I connect happiness with Heaven. I have had good times in this world, but the joy that this world offers is fleeting.

No one ever came back from the grave to tell us what is there, but we know from the vision of St. Paul that it is something that the eye has not seen and the ear has not heard. I think to myself, what is it going to be that the eye has not seen, the ear has not heard? It must be something extraordinary. I know I am going to have a wonderful time.

I pray for a happy death. I am completely submitted. If it is His will that I go today or tomorrow, I will go. I have seen quite a few of our sisters pass on. There is something very beautiful about each one's dying. There is none of this "I don't want to die, I'm afraid to die" kind of thing. They die very peacefully; there is a true submission to the will of God.

I pray to Our Lady that she will be with me and give me courage in the face of death. I pray that my death shall be an inspiration to others so that it may help others to overcome their fear. I am not going to say I am not afraid to die, because that would not be truthful. Even though I am religious, I have not discarded my human nature. I would not be a normal person if I did not have some fear of death. There is a certain kind of fear . . . it is difficult to explain. I guess it is the crossing over, the unknown. We are all afraid of breaking with what we are comfortable with. I think I fear the separation of the body and the soul: what is that moment going to be like? How much pain is there going to be? Because it is a kind of suffering, I am sure the pain will help me shorten my stay in Purgatory.

I am not going to look for streets of gold, and I am not going to look for mansions. I love nature and look for beauty in life here on earth. I think if the world is as beautiful as it is here, what is it going to be like there? I know the kind of peace and joy that I have experienced in the chapel or walking in the hills and talking out loud to the Lord and feeling His presence will be continued in Eternity. There will be the fullest amount of love, the fullest amount of joy, the fullest amount of peace.

I believe I am going to meet all those in my family who have already gone. I am very anxious to meet all those great wonderful people whom I read about and have been inspired by. Above all, I am going to meet the one I love.

I am preparing for my Heaven and my Eternity here on earth. The better I know God here and the more I love Him here, the more I am going to experience His love when I get to Heaven. I know He is waiting for me. I want to prove to Him that I really do love Him. I want to be faithful to Him to the last. I am not afraid of facing the Lord. I sincerely believe I have vowed my life to Him. I approach Him as a bride. I am waiting to go to Him, the one to whom I have given my life. The one I love.

I want to be in His presence. I want to see what He looks like. I expect my Eternity to be one of constant loving, of a building up, a growing, of a developing of that love. If you are in love, who do you want to be with? Do you ever have enough of looking at the one you love? Do you ever have enough of being with the one you love? I do not want to sound like a romantic. I am not in love with love, I am in love with a real person.

I would like to meet the Lord as a lover. I know that is the way I am going to be greeted. I am not fantasizing, I am convinced that is the way I am going to be met in

Heaven. He will say, "I am glad you are here," and we will embrace. And then He is going to show me His Heaven . . . and that is going to take all Eternity.

I do not think this is a wish-fulfillment. I am very much convinced that there is an Eternity. If God is love, there cannot be a nothingness. If God has created us in His image, will He allow that image to just disappear? We have been told by the Lord that He has prepared a place for us, and I am taking Him on His word . . . He can't tell a lie, He's God.

The Obsession

Lenny Cardillo, thirty-eight, lives alone. He is unemployed and collects welfare.

And shall cast them into a furnace of fire;
there shall be wailing and gnashing of teeth.

—Matthew 13:40–42

Once my mother said to me, "The day I married your father, I should have dropped dead." I think to myself, the day you got pregnant with me, you should have dropped dead. You see, I'm a loser.

Most people will tell you that winners and losers are self-made. If you're a loser, it's your own fault. Psychiatrists will tell you that. When a psychiatrist doesn't have any answers, you know what he says? It's your own fault. I don't believe that. You don't choose your life circumstances.

In grammar school I was always the class weirdo. High school was a nightmare. I can't become less neurotic until I have better dealings with people, and I can't have better dealings with people until I become less neurotic. It's just a vicious cycle. There is nothing that is going to change my personality and make me more like other people—nothing short of a miracle. Now, who's going to perform that miracle? A psychiatrist will tell you you've got to perform that miracle yourself. You have it in your power to exorcise all these demons. You have the magic wand. Wave it.

There is no hope for somebody like me. I am out of sync with the rest of the world and always was. I think suicide is heroic. I envy people who can do it. Once I actually had the pills in my mouth. If I knew for sure, absolutely sure, that when you died there is nothing, just like before you were born, nothing—no joy, no pain, no suffering, just nothing—I would have done it; I would have done it long ago. I'd do it now, I would, I really would . . . only that thought has always stopped me.

I am an agnostic, a born-again agnostic. I am totally confused as to God, the devil, the hereafter. When I was a teenager, I had a strong belief in what I was taught. By the time I was in my twenties, I think I lost it. My intellect tells me that all these religious teachings are bullshit, but my emotions overrule my intellect. I can say, oh, that's ridiculous, think intelligently, think logically; but that doesn't do any good. Would you be afraid to be alone in a room with a corpse? What does your intellect tell you? There is nothing to fear, that dead body is just going to lie there. It's not going to get you, it's not going to hurt you. But what do your emotions tell you? They play tricks on you, right?

You see, I intellectually understand that these thoughts are only the demon guilt that is tormenting me, but that is no relief.

*   *   *

I was brought up a Catholic and attended Catholic schools. All I know is if I had children, I wouldn't let them go within ten miles of a Catholic school. The nuns would teach you that you are supposed to love God and that's your reason for being good; and yet, at the same time, they are telling you that the real reason, the main reason, for being good is so you won't go to hell. That is sort of a contradiction.

One thing the nuns used to say all the time that sticks

out in my mind is, "Use your brains. God gave you brains, use them." I would think to myself, if I'm using my brains, that means I should question what you're telling me about God.

I remember when I was ten years old. There was one nun who was very strict. She had a reputation for being hot-tempered and very mean. I had her for fifth grade. She would always say that the alternative to being good was Everlasting Fire. There were illustrations in our Catechism books, and one was a man kneeling in fire, with his hands over his face like he was sorry about his sins, but there was no longer anything he could do.

Once she said, "If you steal something, you have to give it back or replace it. If not, you will burn in hell." I think I had stolen something very small. I got panicky, fearful. It became an obsession—I'm gonna go to hell . . . I'm gonna go to hell.

It was so bad and I was so nervous that my mother had to take me at night to the convent to speak to the nun. My mother explained to Mother Superior that I was nervous and that I was having problems. This Mother Superior was very nice. She was an exception. She called my teacher, and my teacher and I went alone into the chapel. We talked maybe an hour. She told me not to be nervous. I remember I mentioned masturbation to her. She said it was a mortal sin and that it was impure. Up until then, I thought the only reason not to masturbate was because it was disobeying your parents. It was the first time anybody made me associate it with impurity.

No child is born with those fears. I wasn't born with those thoughts about hell. They planted it. Because I was so sensitive and had such a vivid imagination, I was a fertile field for it to grow. They planted the seed in me, and then it blossomed.

*   *   *

I have a horrible guilt complex. But what am I so guilty about? I don't think I deserve punishment, but I think I'm going to get it anyway. I feel I'm no worse than the average person. I look at other people and I say, they have sinned, just like me; but they have nothing to worry about, though *I* have to worry. Everybody else is going to be judged fairly, everybody except me, because I am such a loser.

Recently, when it's gotten bad, I've talked it over with my mother. She tries to understand. She tells me, "You're not bad; you're not going to be punished. What have you done?" But I know this. I realize all these feelings are irrational, and yet I can't do anything about it . . . Oh, God, what can I do.

If I really concentrate on it, it becomes more and more frightening. I think to myself, you know, if you go on this way you will become insane. Then I think, well, maybe insanity will be better than this.

It's like having a supernatural presence constantly hovering over me, and this supernatural force is saying to me, "I've got it in for you; I'm out to get you. I can read every minute thought you are thinking, I can pick up every minute action you perform. I've got it all ready for you. You are going to feel fire. You are going to feel cold. Every horrible thing that you feel on earth, you will feel—but worse."

Why would any supernatural force be so concerned with me? There are millions of other people on this earth to be concerned with. There are millions of other problems on this earth and other planets. Why me? I'm like a grain of sand on a beach; one little grain of sand. Why did he pick me?

I think to myself, what is this supernatural force? Is it God? Is it the devil? Then a funny, horrible thought comes to me: maybe God and the devil are one and the same— Dr. Jekyll and Mr. Hyde. Then I say to myself, that means the winners are created by God, and the losers are created

by the devil. So *I* was created by the devil. No matter what
I do, I am condemned.

Something has to trigger it off. It could be anything, just
an everyday occurrence. I'm outside in the cold, and I say
to myself, just suppose I had to be out in this horrible cold
for eternity. Or, I'm at the stove and I burn my hand. I
think to myself, well, suppose you had to have that burning
sensation for eternity? Then I think about it, and I think
about it. It becomes an obsession.

I invent my own hell. What I was taught by the nuns
wasn't so bad as how I conceive it to be. They said you'd
be in a lake of fire with all the other sinners. To me that
isn't bad enough; at least you're with other people. I'd have
to be in that lake of fire myself. My hell is always lonely.
Being all alone for eternity and calling out . . . and nobody hears me.

The Politics of Immortality

Curtis Henderson,* fifty-five, was co-founder and president of the now-defunct New York Cryonics Society. The Society was founded in 1965 to encourage and promote interest in aging research and the development of the technology for freezing people after death in order to preserve the body until technological means are devised to restore life.

For some reason, the human race is engaged in a great deception of itself. You see it all around you. There's no sane way to explain the situation that the world has gotten itself into. I think a great number of people just feel overwhelmed by all these forces around them—that it's just a matter of time before they're on the Bowery washing windshields.

I guess at times I've had that feeling myself. There doesn't seem to be any reason or meaning to life. I think that disturbs people. People seem completely unwilling to accept the concept of uncertainty. There is a need to build a structure, a philosophy; otherwise, this great successful business of religion would not have come along. I think it's just an attempt to put what's basically a very disordered world, a world people can't understand—and maybe it's not understandable—into some kind of framework they can deal with.

I don't think anybody really believes in heaven or hell. The world certainly would be a different place if they did. I see no evidence of an afterlife. I've known a lot of people who have died; and if they could come back and haunt me, I'm sure they would.

People say they believe in an afterlife, but why do they run to the doctor when they get sick? Why do they go to church to pray to get well? Why don't they hurry on to

162

their heaven? They don't believe in it either. Nobody believes in it. Nobody.

As to why people conjured up the afterlife . . . as they say: No man can look at the sun or death directly in the eye. They just don't want to accept the concept of a world in which you grow old and die.

Death holds no fascination for me whatsoever. I don't consider myself in an eye-rolling state of panic at the thought of death . . . I just cannot see it as anything pleasant. What is it that Mark Twain said about growing old: The alternative is still worse.

I view religion—particularly since this Jonestown fiasco— with a jaundiced eye. I have no objection to people believing in God, and I won't argue religion with people. Why go around trying to prove there is no God? I don't know if there is one or not. All I know is he hasn't spoken to me, and he hasn't told me to lead the people to Guyana or anyplace else.

*   *   *

I buy a lot of books. I used to get the Sunday *New York Times* for the Book Review section and use the rest of the paper for painting automobiles. I read a review of *The Prospects of Immortality* by Robert Ettinger. I guess this was in 1964. I went out, bought the book, and read it.

I wrote to Ettinger and he sent me back the names of some people in New York City, and I arranged to meet them; one was Saul Kent. I had a very good job at the time; I worked for an insurance company. I could do my job in two days a week and spend the rest of the week on my boat.

I don't usually write to anybody or join anything. Causes to me . . . they're all lost causes. This was really a lost cause. Political causes are meaningless to me—one day the Japs are your enemies, and the next day you're riding in a

Honda; did anyone really think we were fighting for apple pie and baseball?—but this one was different. What do you want me to tell you, that I was at a cocktail party and I said, God's no good, lightning struck, and there it was, the Cryonics Society? It just didn't work out that way.

I got into this for the selfish, mean reason that I don't want to grow old and die. This to me was real. If this could be done, it was worth making an effort. This was worth changing my lifestyle. I think Gore Vidal said it: "After you're thirty, don't look in a mirror." I agree. I'm just like a vampire; I stay away from them. I don't look in the mirror, so I don't have to suffer that indignity. Aside from a bottle of vodka, there is no way you're going to make old age acceptable to a person like me. Other people may say, Well, it's nice to grow old and sit out on the porch. I don't like sitting on a porch, and I'm going to avoid old age and death if I possibly can. If I can't take it with me, I ain't goin'. It's as simple as that.

*   *   *

Once Saul and I got into this thing, it became a great adventure. The ultimate goal was always way beyond the horizon; it just was the sheer adventure of it that carried us along.

You know that ratty little paper *The Enquirer*? They had a great big spread: Doctor So-and-So was freezing bodies in Russia. So we wrote to him. It was quite a thrill getting a letter back with a hammer and sickle on it. It turned out that he wasn't freezing bodies; it was just something that somebody from *The Enquirer* had made up. A guy from the CIA came the next day and wanted to know all about it. I said to him, "What do you want? I thought you guys only worked outside the country."

"We're just interested."

Then he said, "Well, do you think they're freezing bodies in Russia?"

I told him, "That's what I'm paying you to find out."

All these people said they were freezing bodies. There was this guy who said he had a secret body facility in Cleveland; another man, named Gold, said he had one in Springfield. There was another guy in Kansas City who said he was freezing bodies; and there was a man out in Arizona, Hope, who said he was freezing bodies. All these people would talk, and we'd just listen.

To find out if these people really existed, I used the credit check system. For $5 you could find out a man's address. One day Saul said, "We're gonna get in the car and we're gonna go to all these places and find out what's really going on." It turned into being like a Batman and Robin adventure.

We arrived in Cleveland at a place called the Ryan Tank Company. It was owned by a man named White who was making cryogenic tanks . . . but this had nothing to do with freezing bodies.

We got to Springfield, and when we went to the address that we had, we found an abandoned shoe factory. We were sitting across the street just looking at it when—you're not going to believe this—a man pulled up in car and said, "You guys are looking for the place where they freeze bodies." He handed us some crudely drawn plans and said, "Here are the plans for the Cryotorium."

We heard that Gold had attempted to freeze bodies. We went to the newspapers and looked through their files. We found a reporter who had covered the incident. Gold must have been a very remarkable man; he convinced this reporter that he was going to get a Pulitzer Prize for covering this story. This reporter had written it up and put it on the front page of the *Springfield News* for several days. Gold had bought this tank from some outfit named Cryo-Vat, and he was going to freeze this woman. By that time, I had already learned enough about cryogenics, and the story didn't ring true to me. We went back to the deserted factory. The place was in bankruptcy and all fenced off. We went over the fence and into the factory. We found the tank . . . it was a fake.

From there we went to Kansas City. The address we had turned out to be a dummy office; we found that the real address was a funeral home. We knocked on the door and said we were from the Cryonics Society and we wanted to find out if they were freezing bodies. With conspiratorial looks, they asked us in. They began showing us all these color pictures. I don't know what they were trying to sell us . . . but they, too, weren't freezing bodies.

When we got to Phoenix, Arizona, Hope had a woman frozen in a tank. I don't know what ever became of her.

*   *   *

In the beginning, we never intended or expected to freeze bodies ourselves. What happened was a man named Nelson started a cryonics society in California. There was a professor named Bedford; he had cancer and he had money. He put up the money—I think it was $200,000—and said, "When I go, freeze me." So it was put up or shut up.

The logic of freezing bodies is to stop somebody from deteriorating after death. You freeze somebody because they have a disease that you can't cure, on the theory that when you have a cure for the disease, and you have the technology for reversing the death process, you can bring him to the stage you froze him at.

It's just putting somebody in a refrigerator, only you're using an expensive refrigerator and a very low temperature. All it's going to do is keep you from rotting. It's not going to make you young again, or cure the disease you've died of; it's not going to perform any miracles.

What we really wanted was a Manhattan-type project directed at stopping aging. We really felt that aging research was far more important than freezing bodies. If you don't stop aging, even if this freezing thing does work, and the technology to reverse the death process is developed, it will probably be the most painful, expensive, complicated medical procedure that could be conceived of. It's like uncooking an egg.

Now, you bring somebody back who is seventy-five years old; he can't hear, he can't see, he can't taste . . . he'd probably strangle you. You aready have movements that say stop all this fancy medical technology that is only prolonging the agony. I agree with these movements. I think it's ridiculous to spend hundreds of thousands of dollars to keep somebody, who is eighty-nine years old and nothing works anymore, alive.

In the days that we began the Cryonics Society, we used to go to gerontology conferences. You'd see the old men up there, fumbling around, dropping their false teeth on the floor, and talking about growing old gracefully. It can't be done. There's no growing old gracefully. There's nothing dignified about growing old. Anybody who says that is just talking. You don't grow old gracefully—you start to fall apart.

Everybody's just kidding themselves. The cosmetic industry makes billions. They're spending all this money on nursing homes. Health care is the biggest industry in the world. Social Security—a third of everybody's paycheck—for what? To add some uncomfortable years to the end of your life? It's just craziness.

I don't see how medical science can look itself in the face unless it addresses this thing. All medical science is nonsense if it doesn't stop aging. But you don't have medical science; you have medical business. All this money that is spent by women today to raise their faces; all these doctors are getting to be millionaires by doing face lifts. They can make people look younger . . . for three more years, five more years; all of this is addressed at the problem, but it's as if they don't want to pull the knife around and go for the real jugular.

*   *   *

We never got any attention or publicity until this body freezing thing came along. The media saw only this body freezing thing, and it was blown up and made into something it wasn't. I really have a feeling that the fascination with freezing bodies was more of a media event—a chrome-plated, souped-up, Dracula-type idea. They were fascinated with the idea of somebody getting out of a coffin, and they weren't going to be happy until I turned into a bat and flew off.

You want to know why the bodies were wrapped up in Reynolds Wrap like a Sara Lee pie? I'll tell you why. A British magazine came by here one day when we first started and said they wanted to do something on this idea. When we finally got a hold of the magazine, they had a picture of a beautiful girl wrapped in Reynolds Wrap with just her face showing. It looked real good . . . so from then on the bodies were wrapped in Reynolds Wrap.

The way this whole thing was snatched up by the media, I couldn't believe it myself. I can't explain it to you, because I can't even explain it to myself. I had a guy who was helping me in the warehouse loading and unloading these cryogenic tanks. One night on TV there was a "Star Trek" episode where they found a rocketship full of frozen bodies. Later that night, he turned to me and he says, "You know, Curt, they're really freezing bodies. I saw it on 'Star Trek.'" Now this guy had been right there with me when we did it.

I went along with this body freezing thing. (Went along? —we were carried along.) There wasn't much we could do. Things just kept happening. To the degree we directed them, I really don't know. At our stage of the game, we were really guerrilla theater. I didn't think anyone had a chance of coming back, and we told people that.

The original idea was that somebody would join the society and either set up a trust or buy an insurance policy, and when they died they would be frozen. A lot of people joined and said they wanted to be frozen, but nothing ever came of it. It never worked in the sense of a formal situation. With the exception of Bedford, I don't think anybody's been frozen who consciously made a lot of arrangements.

What usually happened in almost every case is that when somebody died, one of the relatives would decide that they wanted to do this. Of course, the call always came at four o'clock in the morning: "My father just died and I want him frozen." You'd say, "Well, you know, it costs a lot of money; there's a lot of problems."

"I don't care. I want him frozen."

Technically, if you're going to freeze somebody, you should get him practically at the moment of death. The body should then be profused with some sort of cryo-protective agent. They never would call you before the person died. The body was always in some hospital, in Washington or some place. You would explain to them that the funeral director's got to go there and make arrangements, and before you know it, $2,000 will be spent. Then you gotta get the body on dry ice and that's expensive. Then I'd explain: You've got to order a tank; the tank has to be made individually each time, and it usually takes between six weeks to two months. I didn't want them ordering the tank and then not paying for it. I'd say, "Well, the tank costs about $5,000."

"I don't care, I want him frozen."

They say that then, but when the time comes to pay for the tank . . .

You'd start the process going and then the rest of the family would find out. There was usually a family fight because the others weren't willing to spend the money. These things seem funny looking back on them, but they weren't funny. They were really very sad.

One of the problems with the whole freezing thing is that when you come into a death situation with a family, you're talking about something that can be done; whereas in a normal situation, nothing can be done. Everybody just stands around and looks sad, then they go home and go on dealing with their lives. If you take this route, you're just not going to go home and go on with your life.

It's gonna cost a lot of money. After you've paid for the tank and paid for all of the traveling and monkeying and the shipping and ice, I would say today—if you're going to do any sort of decent profusion job—you're talking about something in the neighborhood of $20,000 to $25,000. Then you're talking about probably a couple to $300 a month after that for maintenance.

Now what usually happens is people just get tired of paying the money. Their lives go on. Things change. The individual who is frozen is fading in their memory, and here's all this money going out. What can you say to them? I mean, is the body ever going to be brought back? What are the chances? Now they really begin to reflect on what they've gotten into.

I really begged people not to get into this unless they really could afford it without it being any kind of a burden. I'd tell them, "Look, you're getting into something that's going to go on indefinitely. You're going to be paying; and if it's going to be a financial burden, you're going to reach a point when you're not going to want to do it anymore, which means everything you've done up to that point— if you'll pardon the expression—will rot."

As far as this body freezing thing is concerned, I think the chances of coming through it are so slim that they're not worth anybody making big sacrifices. Now, if a man has millions of dollars, that's one situation; but if some guy's working in a factory for $110 a week and is trying to keep his father frozen, that's another situation. I wouldn't do it. Ettinger would gasp if he could hear me. His policy was freeze 'em no matter what. But he was never in the trenches. He never froze anybody.

The amazing part of all this is that Ettinger was convinced that after the first man was frozen, everybody would see what a wonderful idea this was and it would really go . . . but it didn't. Over the period of time when we had the facility here on Long Island, and we could do it reasonably well, there were very few people that wanted to freeze anybody. We froze seven people, and I think only two remain frozen today.

The Cryonics Society of New York was financed mostly out of the pockets of Saul and myself. Nothing will keep going unless—to put it bluntly—it makes money. We found we were going broke. Cryonics wasn't making any money, so we had to go about our business.

*   *   *

When we started, everybody was sure that the whole world would see how great this idea was and would take it up: Big companies would provide the equipment, big cemeteries would open cryotoriums, and so on. But that simply didn't happen.

If you ask me why people like the Rockefellers sit around, do nothing about aging research, and just simply grow old and die—I can't give you an answer. What wretched little research has been done indicates that there is no reason why people should grow old. It shouldn't take a hell of a lot to stop it . . . yet all of these rich and powerful people drop dead left and right.

If you ask me why the whole medical establishment isn't

concentrating on stopping aging, I cannot tell you why, any more than I can tell you why the whole military industrial complex is concentrating on blowing us all up.

You live in a society of engineers who can't start their cars in the morning, lawyers who pay their first wives alimony, and doctors who die. That doesn't mean that you're never going to start the car in the morning, it doesn't mean that you're always going to pay alimony, and it doesn't mean that you're certainly going to die. Sometimes the car does start, sometimes you don't pay alimony. Now we got the third one to deal with.

We all have a terminal illness. It's just a matter of time. All you gotta do is walk into a savings bank, give them your age, and ask them what they want for savings bank life insurance. Very quickly you will get a nice little computer read-out on the odds of how many years you've got left. Now, it's always a shock to people; nobody wants to think about it. Life insurance companies think about it. They know the statistical probability of your living almost to the day.

When you're young, you don't think about it. But one of these days, you're gonna be going along, and you'll meet somebody you haven't seen in twenty years; and you're going to say to yourself, geez, he looks like death. And you're gonna realize—whether you do it consciously or not I don't know; but deep down inside you there's a little light that's gonna light up and say, you look just as old to him as he does to you; and a little bell will ring reminding you that the clock is running.

Will we just sit here and accept that we are all terminal cases, or will we do something about it? Now, maybe it is incurable; maybe it won't be cured in your lifetime . . . but then again, maybe it will. Surely this business of growing old and dying is the biggest personal problem you have.

You have to address medical science and get them to try to accept the concept that there is no more reason why people should grow old than they should catch the black plague. Now I'm sure when people were dying left and right of the bubonic plague, there were those who sat around and said, well, if it hits you, that's tough; you've got to accept it, die quietly and don't make any trouble.

One of these days you will get medical science interested in stopping aging; I firmly believe this. But it's one of these things that takes forever and ever to get people really interested. Going to the moon when I was a teenager—this was a sure sign of craziness; this was the ultimate in insanity. They spent more money on science fiction stories about going to the moon than they did going to the moon.

The concept of immortality is really not so off the wall. I personally feel there is a very good chance that if more research is done on aging, it can be arrested within the next ten . . . twenty . . . forty years. It doesn't have to be totally arrested; say you just slow it down a bit. That gives you another ten or twenty years for it to be arrested. To me, this would be the greatest scientific technological triumph you could possibly have. This is really going to turn everything around. It is going to be the *real* revolution.

Whether that's good or bad, I don't know. I have no idea what kind of civilization people who stay eternally young are going to have. I haven't the foggiest idea. I can foresee all kinds of battles and conflicts, but they're going to be there anyway. The only difference is that you're still going to be young and healthy.

When you think about it, all the Social Security, all the plans for old age, all this money, all this human energy that is directed at taking care of old people, is going to be turned loose. It also means that those groups who stay young and healthy indefinitely are going to be much richer, much more powerful, and are apt to do away with those who are not. This, of course, is what's been going on all along anyway. I mean look at what happened to the American Indians.

You talk about social problems—these are other people's problems. I'm selfish. I'm really not interested in other people's problems. I'm not interested in the starving Chinese. I really don't care about them; but I do care about whether I grow old. When it comes down to a gut interest, my gut interest, like everybody else's, is in myself.

Are you really worried about the population explosion? Are you willing to die to save some unborn Chinaman? You can contribute to the solution at any time by blowing your head off. It just isn't true; people are not willing to die to make room for untold generations in the future. They're not even willing to spend a nickel.

I don't understand why people today are so shocked by my attitude. I don't think *they* really care either. These are things you are taught to worry about. You're really not worried about the population explosion. Get a toothache—see how long you worry about the population explosion; get old, get locked up in one of these nursing homes. . . .

I know the younger generation has been brought up to believe in this altruistic, misty, "I have a dream" world . . . well, I wasn't; and I know there is no such world. Whether you like it or not, the population problem is probably going to be solved the way it always has been solved—we'll kill each other.

Is there such a thing as social cost? That is a very strange concept to me. I don't know what social cost is. It's a meaningless statement. I'm not going to listen to a lot of nonsense about the economic effects of it some hundred years from now, because you don't know what it's going to be like. You wouldn't have anything if everybody started worrying about what the social cost would be. C'mon, what do you want—an environmental impact statement on staying young? In order to avoid any possible social costs, I should forget the idea of staying young indefinitely? I know damn well if there is a pill available to keep people young indefinitely, it's gonna sell, man. Nobody's gonna worry about the social costs.

Maybe I'm just an old fogey, but there's something that I've never been able to understand. I remember during the Vietnam war I saw all these kids out there screaming and yelling, "Stop the war." And all anybody was worried about was what was going on in Vietnam. They weren't the least bit concerned about the fact that their government was mortgaging their future for all time. They didn't seem to be the least bit concerned about the beginning of inflation. Perhaps they just didn't understand what it meant, I don't know; but when you tried to talk to them, they had memorized these phrases like, "Hey, hey, hey, LBJ, how many kids did you kill today." Meaningless nonsense in my mind. Hey, hey, hey, LBJ, how much bigger in debt did you put us today. That's how I felt about it. You see, I'm selfish; I'm thinking about me.

I don't think anybody joined the anti-war movement because they were against the war. I think they just wanted to join a movement. It's like what Napoleon said about the French Revolution: It was caused by vanity. Liberty, equality, fraternity, and all that stuff—well, they just thought that up afterwards. I don't think anybody even knows what these things are. They are just catchwords people use to get other people to join movements.

I don't think anybody has any idea what the good of mankind is. I'm in no position to determine it, and I don't think any government is in any position to determine it. I see no promise that Cryonics is going to improve human nature nor is it going to enhance the "brotherhood of man."

*   *   *

I think we've planted the seeds of this thing. All around the country there are young people going into the sciences, and in the back of their minds they're consciously heading towards stopping aging . . . not for humanity, not for some mystical good or social benefit, but because they don't want to grow old.

Our whole program was to push as many small cryonics societies in as many locations as possible. Well, it worked in a sense. There's California, Michigan, Florida. There's one in Australia, one in France, and there's one in England. Now they're probably all just two men, a dog, and a mimeograph machine . . . but they're there. That's something.

I can't answer the question why people accept growing old and dying. I can't understand why there isn't an aging program. I can't understand why people who have a lot of money don't arrange to freeze themselves . . . I guess they're afraid they're doing something out of the ordinary and people are going to laugh at them. You know, it's the same old story: Indoor plumbing really got going when Grover Cleveland put a toilet in the White House.

6
War

Then conquer we must, for our cause it is just
And this be our motto: "In God is our trust!"
And the star-spangled banner in triumph shall wave,
O'er the land of the free, and the home of the brave!

—Francis Scott Key

The Game

Bob Perry, twenty-eight, is an automobile mechanic.

The games of children are their most serious business.
                                        —Montaigne

When you're a little kid you play army. It's fun to have your gun and shoot the other guy. No one gets hurt; it's just a game. I think a lot of guys think war is gonna be the same way. You're gonna have your gun, you're gonna go out there, see some guys, and you're gonna shoot 'em. No chance of you gettin' killed.

I guess I wanted to do something, that's why I joined the service. Seeing a war on TV, it seemed exciting to go out there. I just wanted to go and fight, just see what it was like.

In the Marine Corps we were very gung-ho. I remember my D.I. telling me a story how they caught a whole platoon of NVA in a river: "Only their heads were sticking out. It was just like shooting pumpkins. You know what, after a while we really started to enjoy it. We were havin' the best time just shooting these guys. When you go over there, after you get your first or second kill, you're going to start to enjoy it."

The first day I got to Vietnam, when I got off the plane, I was really scared. I just stood there and said, "Shit, I could be shot." But that was the only time it ever entered my mind. After you're in the country for a week, you think nothing of it. It never entered my mind being blown away or shot. I guess I sort of always had this idea in my head that it's always gonna happen to the other guy.

Where we were stationed there really wasn't any action, and I got bored sitting around every night not doin' nothin'. It was very frustrating having an M-16 and just looking at it every day and not being able to fire it. I wanted to go out there and shoot at something.

I volunteered to go out into the field at night. We'd get into fire fights; we'd be launching rockets into the air and all this stuff, and I'm shooting my rifle and having a good time. The next morning, we'd get up and go back to the base and it would be all over with. I was out there having fun. The war didn't seem real to me. It was more or less like a game.

It's sorta like a lot of things you do in life. Like having your first cigarette. You do it because the other people are doing it, not really because you need it. Then you start enjoying that cigarette, you know, and then you need that cigarette. It's the same thing with killing. It's kinda like having your first drink. You do it because other people are doing it. You get sick, but after a while you say, hey, I do it and I enjoy it.

Like I said, the war wasn't real to me. It was nothing but a game.

War Wounds

Jeff Miller, thirty-two, is a trust officer in a bank.

"Forward, the Light Brigade!"
Was there a man dismay'd?
Not tho' the soldiers knew
Some one had blunder'd.
Theirs not to make reply,
Theirs not to reason why,
Theirs but to do and die.
Into the valley of Death
Rode the six hundred.

—Alfred Lord Tennyson

I remember seeing a war movie when I was a kid. Robert Mitchum played a war correspondent who was trying to find the meaning of war. At the end of the picture he said, "You know why we do this? It's because we like it. When this war is over we're gonna choose up sides and do it all over again."

When I was in Vietnam, I remember talking about that and saying, I think we like this. There's a lot of euphoria in combat. The height of being high is going through a village looking for a guy and knowing if he sees you first, you're dead. Every sense is one hundred percent. I've never taken drugs—but man, that's high. We liked it.

I was a hunter before I went into the Army and I still do a lot of hunting. When you're hunting a deer, you have to see him before he sees you—his sight is better, his scent is better, his hearing is better. The only thing you've got going for you is your mind. You can think better than he can. That pits you against him in equal terms. In combat it's the same thing, but more so.

I think every war probably starts out for some sort of economic reason, but I contend if it wasn't part of our inbred nature we wouldn't do it. It comes from thousands of years of man being a hunter. It's only in extremely recent history that man is what we could remotely refer to as civilized. I think there is a lot of validity in the fact that for tens of thousands of years it has been bred into me. We try to push it down, but I don't think we truly can. When I was in college I used to get a kick out of it when people would make a crack about hunting. They'd say, "You'd probably hunt up people." I used to shock 'em and say, "I tried that too, and it's not bad."

*   *   *

It was 1965. The Mets had just been organized, the World's Fair was on, the Mustang car had just been introduced. Nobody had heard of Vietnam.

I was one of those kids in high school who had a good time. I had a great time, barely got out of high school— and I mean barely. It was by the grace of God that I made it through. I enlisted in the Army four days out of high school.

All I ever wanted to do was be a soldier. I was one of those kids that when everybody was making model cars, I was making model tanks and playing with toy soldiers . . . so it just seemed like a natural extension to go in. I suspect the only reason I wound up in the Army rather than the Marine Corps was because the Army recruiter was a little bit sharper. He fed me Paratroopers, Rangers, Airborne . . . all that shit. And I signed up. I was only seventeen at the time, so I took the papers home, my parents signed, and away I went.

It was still a peacetime Army in '65. My entire basic training was learning how to shoot Ivan. I was in the Army I guess three days when it dawned on me that the way to get through this thing and get ahead was not to do what I did in high school. The way to survive was to keep your mouth shut and do what you were told.

They let me do a lot of the physical things that I enjoyed. I thought running around was a lot of fun, going through an obstacle course was a charge, firing a rifle was neat. What did I know—a dumb seventeen-year-old kid. So I ate a lot of that stuff up.

When I finished basic, I was recommneded to go to an NCO Academy at Fort Gordon. When I completed that, I went on to Advanced Infantry Training. When I got out of AIT, I was asked to stay on as an instructor. By this time, Vietnam was starting to be talked about. The Marines had sent a divsion there and the 173rd Airborne had been sent.

I was instructing on the automatic rifle range. My range officer kept saying to me, "Why don't you apply for Officers Candidate School?" I thought about it, but didn't give it much serious consideration. Until one day . . . It never snows in Georgia, but they have this cold driving sleet in the winter. It was one of those days, and I decided it was no day to go out to the range. So I told 'em that I was going to fill out the papers for OCS.

I wound up going to OCS at Fort Benning in mid-'66, about a year after I was in. I'm only eighteen—shit, I didn't know anything. Up to this point, it was a lot of fun. Again, I made it a point to stay out of trouble. At OCS it was like being a Spartan. It was six months of no candy, no beer, no women . . . no nothing. It was a big thing to get a day off the month before we graduated and go up to Macon, Georgia, and try to find a whorehouse.

I was commissioned as a second lieutenant. I had just turned nineteen. I was a kid—hell, I couldn't even come back to New Jersey and get a beer. All the other officers were twenty-five, twenty-six. It was a unique feeling to know that at age nineteen I was a platoon leader with the 31st Infantry and had total responsibility for forty-three guys. If I wanted to keep them up all night running around their barracks, I could do it. If I didn't want them fed, they didn't get fed. I make no bones about it, I enjoyed it. I had a lot of fun. Women think officers are dynamite even though you might be a nurd. The fact that you got a gold bar makes you cool.

By this time, Vietnam was on everybody's minds; it was in all the papers. The Army had changed its training, and they were gearing people specifically for Vietnam, and they were sending more troops over there. I knew my number was coming up. At the same time, I was very seriously considering a career in the military. So I called up OPO * and said, look, I want to volunteer for Vietnam, and I want to go Airborne Ranger. They said, "Okay, you got it."

I think I had a rather romantic view of war at that time. Fort Benning is the home of the infantry of the U.S. Army. There is a lot of tradition there. There is a sense of professionalism and camaraderie that is not duplicated on the outside. There is this macho feeling that permeates the air: I was with the 31st Infantry, and the 31st has a proud history. They made a big deal over the fact that the 31st was the last regiment to surrender at Bataan. It was E Company of the 31st that went up Pork Chop Hill and they made a big deal over this. It was very easy to get wrapped up in this and forget . . . especially for a young guy who hasn't "tasted" combat.

Death is something you put out of your mind; death happens to somebody else. Since I was a little kid, this was what I was gonna do. I never gave it any other thought.

* Officer Personnel and Operations

I knew that war wasn't as sanitized as it had been when I was a little kid—the wounds weren't as nice and clean—but there was something about it, a sense of duty, challenge, that overrode everything else. You knew what your job was and you accepted it. There was almost a fatalistic attitude among people. I mean, if I was gonna die, I was gonna die a "good old American boy." I knew they'd ship my body back home and plant me in the ground, and that was important to me for what it was worth.

A guy fights for one reason and one reason only—it has nothing to do with Mom and apple pie, the Constitution or any of that bullshit—man will fight because he knows he has to fight, he belongs to an organization that expects him to fight. The guys at the Alamo did not fight and die for Texas independence. They stood and died there because there was a feeling that they had to. Those guys were prepared to fight and die there—period.

The history books are full of examples . . . the Charge of the Light Brigade. . . . I mean it's crazy, it makes no sense, but the feeling is there—that is what is expected of you and that is what you do. You can instill that feeling in people. You gotta work hard at it, but it can be done. The military is good at that. It's easy to psych people up if you have a little experience.

*   *   *

I guess when I first got over to Vietnam I had sort of this macho feeling that some men are born for great things, and I had to make great decisions. When you're out there and being shot at . . . there is no musical background, no great decisions. Somebody's gotta tell somebody what to do, and you're in charge. You simply fly with the best thing you've got. Sometimes you're right and sometimes you're wrong. You hope like hell that the times you are right outweigh the times you are wrong.

Time was lives. You didn't have time to rationalize. The military trains you to react. They take a given set of circumstances and when those circumstances present themselves, you are conditioned to react—period. You couldn't debate whether or not the person you were ordering to move might have a family and kids, or if the person you were going to shoot had a family. You had to put that out of your mind because if you thought about it, you'd go crazy. I was hard on my men though I tried to be fair. Even though I could say jump and they would jump, I would rather have a man jump because he had faith in my decision than jump simply because I had the power of life and death over him.

I remember when I lost my first man. I got a radio call that they had seen action up on this little knoll. I was told to check it out and watch for booby traps. We were walking up a little path at the very top of the hill when my sergeant called me. I went back down and all of a sudden I heard an explosion. It turned out that the guy who was walking in front of me hit a booby trap. The guy never knew what hit him. He took the whole blast in his back. It was a hell of a shot—I mean, he was wide open. It wasn't until the helicopter came in and they put him in a body bag that it hit you: Christ, five minutes ago I was bullshitting with this guy, and now he's dead. . . . It's a strange feeling.

When you're out in the field living with men, eating out of the same C-ration can and passing around the same can of hot beer, you're close, but at the same time you don't want to get *that* close. You have to maintain that distance in your mind, because you know if one of them dies you don't want to be close. I had the somewhat romantic view that every time a man died I was supposed to write a letter to his parents. I told my platoon sergeant, who was an old-timer, what I was going to do and he said, "No, don't do it." I said, "I've got to." He said, "No, let the Army do it. If you do it, every time someone dies, you're gonna have to write a letter, and you're gonna wind up writing a lot of letters. Then you're gonna psych yourself up to the point where you're gonna begin to blame yourself. And if you dwell on that, you're gonna go nuts."

I remember thinking I was gonna get even somehow, but that wears off too. I didn't hate the VC; I found they were good soldiers; I had respect for them. I never went out cutting off anybody's ear or mangling bodies.

You have to put it in your own mind that you're dealing with someone who is not, at least in your terms, human. When a VC was shot and you're going through his pocket for documents and you come across pictures of a family, it brings you back to reality. You killed somebody who has a wife and kids at home just like you do. So I think you have to rationalize, at least in your own mind, that the person you killed cannot feel love or pain. If you wound the son of a bitch, and he gets away, you forget the guy's going to go off in the bush somewhere to suffer and eventually die . . . I mean, you just don't think about that, to protect your own sanity.

We were sweeping a river bed. We had gotten reports that the VC were hiding weapons in the bank. So we're walking down the stream . . . It's about fifteen or twenty feet wide, maybe a foot deep. I got one squad hovering along the sides looking for stuff, and one squad up on either bank just slightly ahead of us for security. So I'm walking in the water . . . not much is going on . . . thinking it's going to be a dull day. I told my platoon sergeant that I was going up on the right bank and walk with the squad there awhile to see what was happening. Just as I got there, I heard an automatic rifle open up. We had busted up an ambush. So I grabbed two guys and started running, figuring maybe we could come around behind them. One of the VC jumped into the stream and starts going across. I could see him through the break in the trees and had a clear shot at the guy. I gave him a burst and stitched him up the back. He didn't go down. I emptied the magazine in him, but he managed to crawl to the bank. I reloaded.

I remember this crazy thought going through my mind: that son of a bitch is going to get away. It was like I was deer hunting, and I was upset this guy was going to get away on me. By the time I had reloaded and was all set to shoot again, he had collapsed. I jumped down between the trees and started wading across after him. It was just an instinct—he went down and I went after him. Goddammit, I'm not going to let him get away.

I walked over to him. He was laying there face up, gasping, and I knew it was a matter of two, three minutes before this guy was dead. I remember taking out my .45 and thinking, hell, I just might as well finish the guy off. I couldn't do it; I just couldn't stand there and blow his brains out . . . I just had to watch him die.

You always wonder when the chips are down whether or not you're gonna produce. Up to that point I never had to produce myself. I didn't do that much shooting; I had to get the other guys to produce. Nine out of ten times I was walking along with a compass and a map trying to figure out where the fuck I was. My killing was always by proxy. This time it wasn't . . . this time it was me.

I remember a feeling—not of euphoria, but of a sense of accomplishment. It's probably an awful thing to say, but that was my job. I trained for that. I didn't think of it as murder. I mean, I didn't kill the guy to take his money; I didn't kill him because I hated him—it was my job to shoot him. I'm sure if the tables were turned, he would have done the same thing to me. He was simply an enemy soldier—period, the end. I could live with that.

I suppose a lot of the feeling I had was pushed under by my responsibilities. I've had a number of experiences where if I was allowed to dwell on them, they would have affected me, probably very adversely. But the fact that I'm standing there and a few minutes later somebody comes up and says we gotta start moving, I don't have time to dwell. I gotta start moving; I've gotta make sure the flanks are secure; I got at least two VC that I know got away . . . are they still in the area . . . are they laying for me . . . are they just the vanguard of a big unit . . . I've got a lot of things to worry about, so it's easy to push it out of my mind. I've got to think. I don't have time to worry about shooting one dumb guy.

One of our companies caught an NVA battalion in a village on the coast. There were mountains popping up on either side of the village. My company was put on top of one mountain, and another company was put on top of the other. They ran tanks along the beach, and they put another company on the highway. They blocked them in on all sides. I sat there that night and just watched them bomb the everloving shit out of that village. They bombarded with naval guns, field artillery; Navy pilots came in all night and bombed. When dawn broke, my company got the order to sweep into the village. My platoon was the lead platoon to go in.

The place was absolutely decimated. There were pieces of bodies all over the place. I remember seeing the upper half of a torso, and as I looked past that I saw a woman. She was rocking back and forth. She was not singing—I guess you'd have to call it chanting. She was holding a dead baby in her arms.

She was the only live person we found in that village— the only live person. She had been badly wounded. I tried to explain to the woman with the little Vietnamese I knew that we were going to take her to the hospital, and I was trying to get her to give up the baby. I hadn't been there that long, maybe three months. I had tears coming out of my eyes. My medic who had been over there almost a full tour came up to me and said, "Don't worry about it, Lieutenant, I'll take care of it." I was never so glad in my entire

life to have someone say that. I was just totally disgusted,
but you force yourself to put that out of your mind. I suppose that was the worst thing I ever saw. I virtually forgot
about it . . . until now.

*   *   *

The NVA and the VC wouldn't come down off the mountains anymore. Consequently, we were given orders to go
up and get them. My platoon was the trail platoon. The
lead platoon caught an NVA ambush from behind. The
ambush was set up for the guys down below. It was just
like the movies—walking up behind the enemy who were
looking the other way. It was a turkey shoot. We blew away
maybe a dozen of them.

The NVA that we didn't get apparently took off and
alerted another group who set up another ambush. It was
a perfect ambush; it was beautiful. The lead platoon
walked right smack into it. I guess there were maybe thirty-
five guys in the platoon and they lost twelve right off the
top. I come running up and I'm maybe a hundred yards
behind the fighting. I see the platoon leader and his sergeant. So I said, "What's going on, what the fuck are you
doing here?" He gave me some excuse that the fighting was
too thick. So I made the crack to him, "Hey, man, they
pay you $368 a month to do this shit, get out there and do
it, or resign and get the hell out of here."

There was no way they were going up there. So I crawled
up with my medic and one of my squad leaders. It was an
absolute mess. This was a triple canopy jungle; this is thick
shit. You can't see ten feet in front of you. You don't know
what the hell's going on. It's not like on TV—you don't
know where the enemy is, you don't have the slightest idea.

I tried to make some sort of organization out of this. I
sent two machine gun teams out to the flanks for security.
I sent my squad leader back for all the ammunition he

could get and I brought up another squad for support. All
this time the platoon leader and the sergeant are still way
back there. So I crawled back to them and told them to go
back and set up a landing zone 'cause we're gonna have
wounded to get out.

The enemy was well dug in. We overran several of their
bunkers, and in the course of the fighting I was winged
in the arm—this was a real "John Wayne wound"—and
wounded in the leg. These two wounds were very superficial. I thought it was funny—I really did. I remember joking with my medic that this was a Silver Star performance:
Lieutenant Miller, with complete and utter disregard for his
life, braved intense enemy fire . . .

There was so much going on, you didn't have time to
think. I led another group over a bunker; and as we went
to overrun the next one, there was some VC off to the side
that we didn't see. We had to go hand to hand. I was
stabbed in the other arm and got bayonetted in the leg.
It was a solid thrust, but it didn't break any bones. It wasn't
that bad, and I remember joking with my medic again.
This time I told him I had gone from a Silver Star up to
the Distinguished Service Cross. He said, "No, that's a
Medal of Honor; hey, White House lawn with LBJ."

I went back, grabbed a handful of grenades, and went
with my sergeant to knock out a couple more bunkers. As
he got up to throw the grenade, he took a shot in the elbow.
He yelled, "Live grenade," and I dove for cover. I took
fragments in the leg. I stood up and took a round below
the knee. I remember going down; I was bleeding bad and
I remember thinking that if I stay here, I'm dead. If they
don't finish me off, I'm going to bleed to death. I had to
get to cover. If I got to cover, I'd be okay. I ran about fifty
yards, ducked behind a tree, and passed out. I remember
waking up maybe twenty-five yards behind the actual shooting. My medic told me he went and got me.

In the hospital in Japan my initial reaction was, I got

to get back, my men are there. If you're a soldier, the place to be is where the fighting is; that's your job, that's what you were trained to do. For a draftee, if he was going home with a "John Wayne wound" and a nice Purple Heart, dynamite; I'm sure he couldn't have been happier. But I considered myself a professional soldier. I didn't want to be doing logistics, playing with schedules, or riding around in a jeep on an Army base. I wanted to be out there to face that challenge where the rubber meets the road.

My leg was amputated two months later. I remember thinking to myself, I will allow myself a little self-pity. I wallowed in it for about forty-eight hours and I said, that's it, no more of this shit. You simply have to live with it. It's over. You know, I think I was more hurt by the fact that my military career was now kaput. My life had ended, so to speak. I mean, here I was, a twenty-one-year-old washout.

*   *   *

When I came home, I spent a weekend in New York City. I was standing on a corner in my uniform, on crutches, with my pants flapping in the breeze. An old lady comes up to me and makes some crack about me being a baby killer. The old lady almost ate my crutch. I almost shoved it down her throat.

I was a soldier and I liked to consider myself a soldier in the best sense of the word. I didn't consider myself a baby killer. As a soldier, your job is to kill enemy soldiers, and I was good at killing enemy soldiers. I killed a hell of a lot more of them than they did of me. My job was not to shoot three-year-old babies; my job was not to gun down decrepit old men. Now, if it's a woman or a ten-year-old kid, and if they're carrying an AK-47 rifle, they're soldiers and they die.

People didn't understand. It was very difficult for me to come back after having all these experiences and not be able to talk about them. At least when a guy came back from

World War II, he could get together with three or four other guys and sit down at the VFW and swap lies. That was not the thing to do after Vietnam. You couldn't explain to older veterans your feelings, because they tended to look upon you with suspicion—you're probably a "hippie" or a "drug freak." Hell, I went down to the American Legion and had this old-timer tell me I didn't know what a real war was like 'cause I didn't go "over the top" like he did in World War I. Come on, give me a break; I mean, I got shot at too, pal. The guy probably never got closer to the Hun than Staten Island.

I started college in 1970. My first semester was when those poor kids were killed at Kent State. I admit that was awful; I knew what it was like to see bodies lying there. The thought was going through my mind, Christ, those kids just watched their friends get blown away for absolutely no reason. I was confused; I was searching, trying to find out what was going on here. I mean hell, I went over to 'Nam, got my ass shot up, lost a leg . . . I was trying to piece this whole thing together.

I originally felt that most of the anti-war demonstrators were sincere, but I became disillusioned with the anti-war movement very quickly. It became obvious to me that the average kid was demonstrating because it was sunny out and they had a rock group playing. Nobody demonstrates on a rainy day. Right away after Kent State the student union started to petition to close the school down. All of a sudden it dawned on me: the only reason anyone's doing this is to get out of final exams. What the hell is this? This is crazy, this is stupid. At that point my political leanings were three feet to the right of Attila the Hun.

I felt the war was right. I liked to think that because I had a vested interest—so to speak—over there. To a degree, I got caught up in this "Let's stop Communism, domino theory" thing and I was willing to put my life on the line for my beliefs.

There are damn few people who will take their feelings and put them on the line. If there were just a thousand people in 1969 who said, "I'm not going; put me in jail, I'll go to jail for a hundred years, but dammit, I'm not going," the country would have been forced to make some hard decisions and the war would have ended in six months.

I realized most of the kids were extremely dumb. They asked me dumb questions, like did I ever kill a baby. They'd listen to anything a professor would say—he's a doctor, it had to be true. There was a group of six or eight of us who were combat vets, and we became our own guerilla group. You know, a professor would say something about the war, and we'd say, "Wait a minute, time out, that's bullshit."

Everybody thought they understood Vietnam because they saw it on the seven o'clock news. You don't have the slightest goddamn idea what went on there sitting back and watching a sanitized version of it on TV—you don't touch it, you don't taste it. I couldn't get people to understand. They had these preconceived notions as to who and what I was . . . and after a while you simply don't talk about it anymore.

We all have feelings that nobody understands. When you try to talk about things that happened to you in 'Nam, it either comes across that you're bragging or that you're whining. You can't explain your feelings to anyone, because nobody wants to hear them. I think a lot of Vietnam veterans have taken a bum rap. I hate when somebody tells me that what I did was wrong. I went over there with very honorable intentions. I did what I felt was right, and I refuse to apologize. That's bullshit. I'm not gonna fall over someone's feet and beg forgiveness because I shot the Cong. Maybe the whole thing got botched up, but dammit, I can honestly look at myself in the mirror in the morning when I shave and don't have to feel bad.

The average guy went over there, did his thing, came home, and took up where he left off. He might wake up nights in a cold sweat; he might have some bad memories that periodically come to the forefront of his mind, but generally he becomes a good father, a good family man, and a good member of society. Whether he works in a coal mine or in an office, he simply does his thing.

*　　　*　　　*

When the peace treaty went into effect, all the churches in town started with the bells. I remember thinking the whole thing was a fucking waste and wondering what the hell was it all for . . . you still wonder sometimes.

I think you get wrapped up in the romantic end of it again, if for no other reason than to keep your sanity. You remember the heroic things, not the cowardice that you saw; the proud things, the good things, the camaraderie. Would I do it over again? . . . Yeah, because I met some guys and had some experiences that were good. Sure, war is bad; Vietnam was depressing; but life itself is depressing in many ways.

You put out of your mind the bad things: the feelings of seeing your first man die, knowing that maybe you screwed up; the feelings when you're walking along and a shot rings out and you look over and the guy who you were just talking to is lying there with the top of his head blown off. I remember seeing my friends die; I remember the doctor saying to me that we're gonna have to take your leg off . . . but you put those things to the back of your mind.

The mind has a great ability to adapt. When I talk with other Vietnam veterans, invariably we start talking about some of the funny things that happened, some of the good stories. We never talk about a friend dying, or accidently shooting a woman . . . because your mind does not want to remember that—and you don't.

It's something that's now in the past. If I'm going to survive as a person, I cannot think about the men under my command who died. I cannot think about men that I killed . . . If I do, I'm gonna lose my sanity. You simply let your mind forget, otherwise you're gonna go nuts.

I feel very sad for those whose minds will not allow them to forget, those who have the reoccurring feelings and the nightmares. They are mentally crippled. . . . They are crippled far worse than I.

Ghosts

Roy Hayes, thirty, has had difficulty holding a job since he returned from Vietnam. He is presently unemployed.

Who is the slayer, who the victim? Speak.

—Sophocles

I still get nightmares, maybe once, twice a month. I had 'em every night for a long time, like about six years. I used to sleep with a light on. I would never sleep near an open door and always had my back to the door. Sometimes I get scared and it may dwell on my mind, and I have to pace back and forth and think things out. I never did this before I went there.

The way I feel now is I'm angry. They messed up my life. They put me in a bind where I had to do things I didn't want to do. We went over there to do their dirty work, and what do we get back here—*nothing* . . . nothing but bad memories.

Last summer, we were sittin' out on the porch and I heard this pop. I said, "Wow, somebody got shot." Then I saw it; it just brought back everything like a flashback. Later my wife found me in a corner stooped down and shakin'. You can't leave the past; it'll always be with you.

*　　　*　　　*

You go to war . . . it's just like a new toy you never
played with. I thought it would be fun. Like when you're
a kid you say: Wow, when I get grown I'm gonna do like
my father do, I'm gonna drink. I betcha that's fun to get
high. Or when you're in a school you say, "I can't wait
till I get out and get me a job." It was just somethin' new,
what would it be like? I never did nothin' like it before. I
never been in combat; I thought there was nothin' to it
. . . I thought it would be a beautiful thing.

*   *   *

I was with my unit out in the field when I got my first
sight of a dead man. He stepped on a forty pound mine
. . . all you saw was blood and flesh. We had to stay there
until the grave registration chopper came in. They had
them plastic bags like trash bags that you throw out. They
just picked up what they could, put a tag on it, threw it
on the chopper and took off. I was sick for two weeks. After
that, it didn't bother me no more . . . you get used to it.

The first person I killed was a boy maybe thirteen, fourteen. Why did I kill him? He was a gook—if I didn't, he
would've killed me. It's just like a toss-up: who's gonna
go, me or him? You couldn't avoid it, or you'd go home in
a pine box, or rot out there in the field. I'd rather walk
than go either way.

I went out and turned him over, this thirteen, fourteen-
year-old kid with a gun in his hand. I felt scared, I felt
shaky. It was like comin' home with a bad report card and
you're gonna get a beatin'. It was just that queasy feeling
. . . your stomach drops, you can't eat, everything is just
drained out of you. You killed this boy. You feel it. You
hurt, you suffer . . . and you get used to it.

There ain't a man who was over there who hasn't killed
no kid or woman. Calley was a little scapegoat so nobody

higher up would get caught at it. Instead of Calley going to jail, all the men that be in Vietnam—we all should have gone to jail. I did the same thing he did. As far as search and destroy, I did it three times. We was only takin' orders.

It was like I had a job to do; I had to do it and get it done. Intelligence would go and tell the colonel that there was either Viet Congs or North Vietnamese in the village. So he says, "Make it a search and destroy," and that's what we did. You go in there, destroy, and you search afterwards. And that's all there is to a search and destroy mission.

You kill everything in sight, just eliminate everything. One time, we got on line and just walked. Anything that moved we shot. It was just like a target practice. Everybody takin' potshots at everything, see what you can pick off, that's all. I seen where one guy sat a six-, eight-month-old baby on a tree stump and started takin' target practice. A live baby. If we hadn't got into town for a while, a lot of guys would kill the men off first, and then do the ladies second—after they got done with 'em.

*   *   *

If you wasn't over there and this search and destroy was your first body count, it would blow your mind. How can guys actually do this? You couldn't believe it. It would blow your mind, it would make you go crazy or hysterical. As far as my feelings, there wasn't nothin' to it. You don't feel nothin' for these people. You just think of 'em as nothin' cause you been over there awhile. I been in combat already. I been through the fire fights before. Like I say, you get used to it. There was no feeling, so didn't nothin' bother me.

Were they innocent or were they not? Maybe yeah, maybe no. If you wasn't there, you'd say they were innocent. If you was there, you'd say they wasn't innocent. I can see an innocent five-year-old kid who'll walk up to you and blow you away. I can see an innocent fifty-year-old woman who'll do the same thing. So it's your story against mine.

A lot of guys say, "My buddy was killed over there. A woman came up and just fired a gun at my buddy." An ol' man did it, a kid did it. I seen what they did to my buddy, so hey, I take it back from them. It was just like revenge. You go out there and build your emotions back up again. Like I say, it was just like target practice. It was fun . . . but after a while, it comes back and haunts you.

I just wake up hollerin' and break out in a cold sweat.

7
Survivors

We have provided for the survival of man against all enemies except his fellow man.

—Lyman Lloyd Bryson

The Aftermath

Paula Rosenkopf, fifty-three, escaped from a Nazi forced labor camp in Poland in 1943 and was hidden by a Polish family for the duration of the war. She is one of five who survived that camp.

> *A single death is a tragedy, a million deaths is a statistic.*
>
> —Joseph Stalin

You say six million. The number rolls over your tongue, but do you truly realize what six million means?

I was in a forced labor camp in Poland. I was there for two years before the camp was completely destroyed. One morning about five o'clock everyone was ordered out; we had to lie flat on the ground with our heads down between our outstretched arms. There were about two thousand people. Many were shot on the spot. The rest were hurtled on trucks and taken to the old Jewish cemetery. There they dug a grave and shot everyone.

As the Commandant walked around, a lot of people picked up their heads and would say, "Don't you know me. I did this for you. . . ." He just shot them without further ado.

There were people lying dead all around me. I still couldn't believe what was going to happen. I just became very numb. I didn't think. As I was lying on the ground, I was doing an arabesque in the dirt, just doodling, not thinking of anything. I can remember in so many situations what I was doing, what I was thinking, so vividly, like it was yesterday, and I'm certain not one single thought came to my mind, either for the past or the future.

You disengage yourself, you just remove yourself from the reality. Even if you knew, deep down in your heart, what was going to happen to you, though you saw what was going on—they were shooting people left and right—it made no impression on you. It's like when you see a lot of something: it stops having that full, close meaning. You don't have the time or the energy to grasp it.

It's funny how after seeing a mass killing one life means more to you than the lives of all these people. It is really very strange how you are surrounded by death but you don't realize what it has done to you until you are faced with that one single death.

My sister was there with us and she didn't survive. When they took her away, and she waved goodbye, that brought back all my feelings: the gruesomeness of it, the tragedy of it, the sorrow, the pity. Probably all these feelings were there, but it took one death for you to realize the full impact of what had happened. Then you realized it was not one, there were so many. Then you felt it so deep, and you began to mourn for all these other deaths.

Reflections on a Life Postponed

Earle Stiles, thirty-one, has been a high school teacher for nine years.

> *We only become what we are by the radical and deep seated refusal of that which others have made of us.*
>
> —Franz Fanon

I was born and raised in Newark in the Central Ward. Growin' up, I had no ideas about life, so I had no ideas about death either. It wasn't a bogeyman, and even to this day it's not a bogeyman.

Bein' poor, you get used to your children dyin' on you. They die from some of the dumbest things. Like home remedies. At that time, you could have an ulcer, and what you'd get for it was kerosene and sugar on a spoon. A lot of people were dyin', and what they were dyin' from was ignorance. There were places where people could go to get help, but people didn't know about 'em. They were also psyched out into believin' that even though you be poor, no matter how poor you get, you don't go around beggin' people. You pay your own way. This type of philosophy is instilled in poor people by rich people so they don't have to be bothered by them beggin' 'em all the time.

In order to be afraid of death, you had to be living, and we weren't living. When you're living in a country and you have all the privileges of a human being and are *aware* of these privileges, it's a whole different trip. You might be afraid of death because you have things that make you feel remorseful about leaving the planet: You won't see the beautiful lakes anymore, the beautiful mountains; you won't see the place where your mother and father are buried. When you're a second-class citizen and you don't have anything, you don't miss anything—what could you miss? Like, you had a few little possessions. You know, we had a big console television and an old piece of radio. We had a beat-up old car, but we didn't get out of Newark much. I thought everything I saw on television was a Hollywood prop: Ozzie and Harriet's house, Leave it to Beaver's house . . . I thought all that shit was props.

Even our religion tells us: Don't think about life here 'cause this ain't the real thing. You just have to go through this to get where you really should be. You must prepare to meet your maker; you know, when you get your wings, your cloud, your harp assignment, all that stuff.

Your parents go to church—it's cheaper than the shrink. They go to this "whatever you can chip in" therapy. Where another person might go to an analyst for $50, they go and chip in their $2 on Sunday and the man tells 'em: Sure, you been gettin' your ass kicked all week, but just you wait, you shall inherit the earth. You either got your booze, sex, drugs or religion in order to keep you from takin' your own life.

*   *   *

I was in a couple of gangs, and I got a few scars on my forehead to prove it. Whatever street you were born on, that was your gang. You couldn't go to the swimming pool two blocks away from your house because it was in someone else's territory. You had to put your dime in your mouth or in your sock, and when you went you had your screwdriver, your ice pick, to protect yourself. I remember marching down a street with twenty or thirty guys, maybe eight, nine, ten years old. In gang fighting, it wasn't like we were out there to zip gun or knife somebody; we had 'em all, but basically we were into sticks, bottles and bricks. You'd throw a brick as hard as you could at somebody and yell, "I'll kill you." There was people getting seriously hurt all the time. I knew two guys who were killed.

Even in gang fighting we had rules. No civilians got involved. We'd even stop a fight to let a lady by. People who are supposed to know better fight wars. Now, I couldn't have dropped the bomb on Hiroshima or Nagasaki. (*On civilians?*) Maybe I could've if they trained me to be that way—not to be a thinking human being, just be a tool—but the person who gave that order is worse than us going into any gang fight with chains and bricks.

Growin' up, there was a very heavy syndrome not to be a punk. You'd die before you'd let somebody take you off. If you had to kill somebody you would. Poor people would do things to each other that they wouldn't dare do to people who have means. It's just like respecting Cadillacs. When you come in between two Cadillacs in a parking lot, it's different than pulling in between two ol' pickup trucks.

If your parents sent you out to the store at night, you had to go down there prepared for anything, because didn't anybody have anything, and they would try to get whatever they could . . . your money, your coat. You might have a leather coat, and you walk down the street and somebody says, "Hey, I like your leather coat. I want it, step out of it." See, that leather coat is all you've got. You got no choice but to fight. Now, some people fight for their country, their mother's honor, and things of that nature. You had different ideas that you had to live or die for. You'd fight for what you had.

Just about everybody made a zip gun. That's what club-houses were for. You'd sit in there and get your antennas and old cap pistols, break 'em in half, get your wood and rubber bands, put it all together, and you got yourself a zip gun. The zip gun was only used to protect your mother. It was something that you put in your closet and you'd have it to protect your house from intruders.

We were always afraid of the police. Man, when you saw the police . . . shoot. Like you might tell your kids, "If you get in trouble go and find the nearest cop." I tell my kids that today, but at that time the police was somebody you did *not* want to see. We never saw the police listen to anyone's story. They'd just jump out of their car, pull their sticks, and start kickin' ass. Whatever aggravation they might have had—like you or I might go to the gym to work it off—they knew where to go. They were gettin' their shit off on us.

They would hassle somebody, and if that person reached into his back pocket to get his I.D. or get out a handkerchief to wipe the sweat off his forehead, if he brought his hands up higher than his waist, it was: You're attacking me, and they stepped in. I seen that I don't know how many times— over a hundred. That's what the '67 riots in Newark were about. A taxicab driver made a wrong move and the cops just jumped out of their car and started kickin' ass.

*   *   *

There was a pool hall right around the corner from us. We used to go there and hang around, sit on the cars, 'cause we couldn't go in. I was about twelve, thirteen. Some of the guys would come out, sit around, bullshit with us, tell us about women. That's what was important, that's what you wanted to be—a womanizer. I can remember in the summer sittin' down on the stoop late at night. You'd get fifteen or twenty people sittin' out there, of all ages, from four to twenty; and the old people be talkin' and the young people listenin'. The thing was, other than gettin' that big car, or how well you could fight, was how many women you could seduce—which would make you bad. It was a different orientation than one of becoming a successful doctor or gettin' into the aerospace program, or whatever.

One thing that came out of the riots was that they started encouraging more kids to go to college. At that time, to be black and to be in college—you were some kind of emeritus. You come back to the community and say you're in college, and it's almost like sayin' you *are* a professor. You took on all this power as soon as you got into college. Whatever you thought you should be, that's what you were goin' to be. If you felt you should become a first class citizen, it was just that sudden. You started to say, hey, I am an American and I do know a little bit of somethin' because I am in college. I got as much on the cap as any of these other people my age walkin' around here, probably even more 'cause I been through more shit. I been through shit that they couldn't even survive.

It wasn't no big scuffle for them to go to the school of their choice with everything they wanted or just to *go* to school. There was no way that you could tell me that their fathers worked harder than mine. My father worked in a gas station seven nights a week all year 'round. He was workin' all those hours for $65 a week. We had to call him up on Christmas and New Year's Eve to say Merry Christmas and Happy New Year. Where was his boss? Why didn't his boss come down and work at least one of those nights? There was some people up the hill and my mother used to go in and clean their house. They were payin' her this little bit of money and giving us their old clothes and junk. Now, here's this lady, she had kids, my mother had kids, and my mother's up there 'til nine o'clock. What's happening to us?

When you were a card-carrying college member at that time, it was like you had a license to be insane. We stole. If we wanted a drink, we'd go into a store, and one guy would buy a pint of wine and everybody else would just be takin' everything off the shelves and putting it inside their coats. We'd confront the police, state troopers. You know, you'd be zippin' down the street in a raggedy ol' car, one headlight out; when they'd stop you, you'd just get all hostile. "Why you stoppin' me?" You'd give 'em a hard time.

We did so many things that brought us close to death. Like, you go someplace where you know there's treacherous people. You know there's somebody in there who just might cut you or shoot you, but you go in anyway and start trouble just for the hell of it, for the excitement. I had a couple of guns, and you'd get into shootouts with other people, other schools. You didn't really want to kill anybody, so you'd have a .22 rather than a .38 or a .45. The motto was, you'd just want to stop somebody, so you'd just want to shoot 'em in the knees, let 'em know—don't come too close.

Like, you got a lot of big people walking around in college, and you have to protect your manhood. One of the ways to protect your manhood is to be crazy and let the people know that you will shoot. Like, here you are shootin' a game of pool and this dude twice your size comes in and knocks the balls all over. What do you do? If you walk out, that means you can't never play pool anymore, 'cause everybody that's bigger than you is gonna push you around. One time I was sittin' watchin' a program on TV and some guys come in, all drunked up, and just turn the channels. So I went upstairs, got my piece, put it in my belt, came back down, and turned it back to the program I was lookin' at and sat down. That's one good reason to have a gun.

I was in college because I wanted to make a little more than $150 a week. I was havin' so much fun that I thought I'd graduate, get me a job in industry, work a little bit, get just enough money for food, rent and a little wine, and just keep on havin' a good time. The recruiters from the big industries came down flashin' this twelve grand, fifteen grand. They didn't care what you studied, 'cause they needed ten percent black for their management positions in order for them to keep their contracts with the federal government. So I said, hey, I'd better get in on that.

My thinking started to change when I met this educator from Philadelphia. I listened to him speak many times. He was what we'd call a jitterbug, which means he was a person who came from the corners but now he had his Ph.D. He could run the stuff down on you just plain and simple. Then he'd go from m.f.'s to twenty-six letter words that you didn't know what the hell he meant. He was tryin' to get the bullshit out of the Philadelphia school system. He'd get kids who were out there gang-warrin' and killin' each other and get them into some positive things.

I decided then that I'm not going to go into business just to make money for myself, but I'd go back to the ghetto and teach, and try to get ten people out of there a year—as many as I could—to go into areas they otherwise might not have thought of. To really get a piece of the action, to have a better life and to become aware, so that nothing can be perpetrated against them because of their ignorance.

*   *   *

I really got into teaching. In the beginning I was doing my thing and reaching the kids, but I found out that there was a lot of negative forces out there in education, and they wanted things to stay status quo. There were teachers that were taking advantage of what you would call the "fringe benefits" of the job. Things like teaching fifteen minutes out of forty-two, sexually abusing the female students, having the young brothers sell dope for you . . . stuff like that.

All this overwhelmed me. Like, you see people gettin' away with things for so long that you start thinking, hey, if you can't beat 'em, you might as well join 'em. I started hustling when I figured this shit was ingrained and wasn't going to change no matter what I did. I found that hard work and meritorious conduct didn't get you shit. It didn't get your son a new bike, it didn't get your wife the things she needed.

What I did was single out people that I figured I could manipulate, kids that could talk well. Instead of telling them, why don't you see if you can get into an upward bound program and get into college, become a lawyer or something of that nature, you just pull 'em over to the side and say, "Hey, look here, man, the world ain't right and here's what we're gonna do. Now here's how we can make some money, and you can get some nice leather shoes and you can get a car." You tell the young ladies, "This is how you can get some nice clothes. All you gotta do is. . . ." See, you're workin' with young minds and you put thoughts in their heads when they don't have any sense. You're not concerned whether you're building morals into them, you don't direct them in a positive way, you direct them for yourself and use them for whatever your purposes might be.

I was into some borderline stuff that was really not that illegal. I was gettin' them to sell junk merchandise, like these disco lights. These things used to burn out in twenty-four hours. You'd tell them just to sell these things, don't tell the people that they're going to burn out. You see a family with kids, just take 'em over to the kids, and the kids will make their parents buy 'em. You teach 'em all kinds of techniques so they'll get more money. I used to tell 'em to go over to New York on Canal Street and buy these little bottles. Then go to Woolworth's and get this cheap perfume. Then get some food coloring and mix it all up with some water. Then buy these zodiac symbols, and you glue 'em onto the bottle. You spend around $3 and you make around $30. You're ripping people off. You go around telling people, "Hey, this here's super cologne; this is your sign. Buy this, it'll enhance your love life."

I knew this guy who was a pimp. He had a business here and one in New York. I used to work for him at night. He

2586703308996885508666

had this spot and he told me to just drift through there and make yourself visible, let the women know that you're around. Naturally, I got to know some of the ladies. Their life was rough and they were doing these things to survive.

Betty was into it for her children. She didn't have any skills and this was the only way she could make the kind of money she needed if she had any dreams for her kids. She was from New York, so while she was over here this pimp would pay her rent, give her kids money, and see how they were doing. She was in a car accident. I heard about it and went over to New York to see her. She had a son—he must have been about ten or eleven—she told me he had become attached to this pimp and was hanging around with him. She said that ever since she was hurt he was staying out late and coming home with all kinds of money. She wanted me to talk to the pimp about her son and she told me the spot on 42nd Street where he hung out.

After searching around for him for a little while, I found him in a bar. I kept asking him where Betty's son was. He had been shooting up and was not lucid at all; he was out of it. He said, "The kid was out working, trying to make some money. Everybody's got to survive," you know, all this stuff. Now, some of the people this pimp was hanging with—these light-weight gangster types—thought I was harassing him, hassling him when he was high. So they started talking: If I didn't go outside and leave him alone, they were going to kick my ass, cut my throat, and all this other stuff.

So I went outside, and while I was standing there a car pulled up and Betty's kid jumped out. Then I realized what was going down—he was out there selling himself. So I grabbed him and told him I was going to take him home. He was saying that he had to be a man now and take care of his mother any way he could.

Somebody must have went into the bar and told everybody that I was hassling the kid. They all came out and surrounded me. They started takin' off their belts, pullin' out brass knuckles, blackjacks, and carrying on like that. I had my gun with me so I got ready to pull and start firing. Then somebody threw a punch, I blocked it, rolled out of the crowd, and ran.

*   *   *

On the way driving back, I started thinking about my life. I decided that this shit had to stop. I thought the best thing that I could do to try to stop it was to work with the kids at school. I decided I wanted to do something because I didn't want too many more people to grow up like I did —come through that same bullshit.

What is important to me now is to build up the capacity to use every cell in my brain to absorb everything I can. I want to develop it and hone it into a fine instrument, and use it to motivate and help other people. As far as I'm concerned, that is my purpose for being here. Why did you get this shot? If you're going to ruin this trip, what the fuck were you? You wasted this whole trip.

I've been happy for a few years now. I'm in that positive state and I want to be a positive person when I die.

The Survival of the Fittest

Saul Liebowitz, fifty-one, emigrated to Israel from Poland after the second World War. He fought in the 1948 war in Israel and later came to the United States, where he has worked at various jobs in the garment industry.

The tragedy of life is what dies inside a man while he lives.
                                                —Albert Schweitzer

In my hallucinations, if I had power, I would take what you'd call drastic measures. I would have no doubts, no change of mind. I would know what to do exactly. There would be no compromises of any kind. I would not hesitate to use nuclear weapons. I do not care about the consequences. They didn't care about me, and I wouldn't care about them. I couldn't care less. It would be a joy to me, even if I had to die with burned hair and burned eyes and burned skin . . . I don't care. I am convinced that the human race has no justification to survive at all. It is an evil creation that must be put to an end.

I know I am nothing and nobody. I might sound to you senseless, as if I don't know what I am talking about. In my own little imagination, such fantasies come around. My own little view might sound crazy, the entertainment of a crazy imagination. I apologize if I make no sense. My view means nothing because I am nobody.

I know it is wrong to speak like this. I would be a disgusting idiot to discredit everybody. I have to respect those people who are doing the right thing and not dwell on my own little experiences. I apologize again for my senseless talk. I understand that there are many people of goodwill who dedicate their lives for others. I met such people. I know some people who even died for others.

I know people have a hard time to raise families, to provide for a wife and children, to pay the mortgage, the car. I have no right to discourage anybody from doing anything purposeful and meaningful. If I don't make sense when I speak, it is based on the experiences that have shaped a mind that is not hopeful.

In my own little mind I don't see any hope for the human race. If you are searching for solutions, or some special revelation, they don't exist. Liberals or progressives may preach about justice, freedom and human decency, but it is to no avail. It is impossible to attain. To do anything, to change things for the good, one must have might; but those who possess might are not so eager to change things for the good. They simply want to expand their power and influence. This has been true throughout history. What decides the outcome in differences of ideology is tremendous force and military might.

It is a merciless world; it is a hopeless world. It is impossible because generally people are treacherous and vicious. It is evidently true what Darwin said, that people are nothing but animals. The human being is a ruthless, violent creature. The general disposition of human nature is jealousy, envy, competition and aggression, which creates a tendency in people to get pleasure from seeing others fail in life. Such a perverted human nature . . . so false . . . so deceitful . . . so selfish; if this is supposed to be human civilization, then in plain English, it doesn't deserve to exist.

Nuclear weapons will be used in due time and the destruction will be tremendous. Maybe that is God's design. It is very possible that those weapons were invented by His will because He feels: You have committed these horrors against the nation whose prophets I have commanded to give my message, whom I have instructed to deliver my commandments. If that is what you have done to these people, willingly, intentionally, by design, then this little earth has no right to survive. I am condemning you to perish as punishment for the horrendous crimes you have committed against those helpless people.

If there is no God, it will come to an end anyhow because of the viciousness of people. With all the nuclear devastating weapons, I don't see any hope. One day tensions will rise, pressure will become very great, and they will use them; and if only two people remain, they will pick up sticks and clubs and they will fight each other.

I didn't always have instant aggression in me or a desire to murder or kill anybody. I was educated to believe in God, that everything was guided by God, and that the world was wonderful and people are wonderful . . . but then it all collapsed. You see, it wasn't my fault. The events and sequences of my life brought me to this point. It wasn't a normal life with normal sequences of development. It is all very involved, very involved.

It is human nature that one cannot really understand others. The human mentality is restricted to one's own life, to one's own family, society or nation. It is difficult to understand an event in which one was not personally involved. One would not have a grasp on it unless one experienced it.

I know my stories are to no avail and whatever I say will make no sense. They are not related to pressing daily problems. People are busy trying to make a living, trying to raise families, and normal people have no time for someone like myself.

*   *   *

Usually the average person knows about Auschwitz, Treblinka, Majdanek. They don't know there were one thousand different camps in Poland. In the small towns the German authorities set up many small camps. They packed large numbers of Jews together in ghettos; and step by step, with cold mind and a feeling of joy, were killing them off in each town where they concentrated them. They were merciless and treacherous. It was one of the greatest organized deceits and horrors in human history. There can never be an excuse for it and it can never be forgiven.

There was an air of rejoicing when the Jews were killed. The Poles were happy to be rid of them. Throughout the centuries, this hatred for the Jews has been rubbed into the minds of their children. A Polish child would cry and the mother would say, "Don't cry or a Jew will take you away." If you would look at the women, they had very cold eyes. There was no smile in their eyes, only a deadly look. If you would look at the children—even they had merciless eyes.

We were put into a ghetto along with many other people from surrounding Jewish communities. The German authorities referred to us as *Menschenverbrecher,* human criminals. The ghetto was encircled with barbed wire and was made into an *Arbeitslager.** In December of 1941 the whole area was proclaimed *Judenrein,* which means it was to be clean of Jews. I was thirteen years old.

The German soldiers marched into the camp around Christmas. Beyond the barbed wire we could see the general population going with pick and shovel in order to dig long trenches. The Germans rounded the people up and told us that Moses was going to take us across the Red Sea, that they were taking us to the front line to dig trenches and to build fortifications. That is the way they lied everywhere, that was their style of fun—to speak senseless lies, to deceive and confuse their victims, while at the same time they were digging graves.

Suddenly a commotion was created. Maybe a thousand

* A forced labor camp

people shouted hurrah and began running toward the barbed wire to break through. They started firing at us with machine guns and rifles. The Germans surrounded the whole camp. Many of them with machine guns walked into the camp. They walked very sure of themselves. They were shooting for fun everywhere. It was so inhuman that a human mind cannot picture it. Many fell dead. The dead were lying everywhere. My brother who was running with me was shot and killed. He was five years old.

I ran into a corridor of a house. A fellow by the name of Moishe was standing there with a rifle and was firing at the Germans. In the whole camp there were maybe ten or fifteen people with rifles. A few Germans were killed and some were wounded. I ran up to the attic and there were a few other people hiding there. The Germans walked into the house and were shouting, *"Juden komm herunter, Moses komm herunter."* * They started firing through the ceiling into the attic. You could see the little smoke of the bullets. I was hiding behind the chimney thinking, that's the end, at any moment I might be hit by a bullet. It was unbelievable that I was not cut down.

That night, they set all the houses afire to make sure that the Jews who were hiding would be killed off. The whole ghetto was burning when I ran out. I hid in the woods that night. The next morning I walked up a hill and could see the ghetto still burning. A black smoke covered the whole sky.

I was hiding down by the river. It was very cold and there was no food . . . only ice and snow. I was picking up pieces of ice and licking them when I saw a group of Polish men carrying picks and shovels. I knew one of the fellows and called to him. He said, "What are you doing here? If they find you they will kill you instantly." He told me that they had been digging trenches and he was there and he witnessed the Jews being shot into the trenches. He told me

* Jews come down, Moses come down.

to run or I would be killed. I ran farther into the woods. I stopped to rest, and I saw someone climb out from under a fallen tree. He was only a tiny boy, smaller than I. His lips and his face were all blue.

We walked together through the woods; the snow was up to our bellybuttons. We got to a small village and sneaked into a barn to sleep amdist the straw. In the morning, we would get out while it was still dark and go back into the woods. My body became infested. The lice were crawling around by the hundreds, eventually by the thousands. I would take off my clothes and shake them out, but they would be back again the next day.

Sometimes we stole food. Sometimes we would go into a village, knock on doors, and ask for a slice of bread. Most of the time they would deny us. One time, two women let us come in and they gave us some bread. A man came in with a red face; he was very drunk. One of the women told us to run, that he wants to kill us. We ran towards the woods and he chased us with an ax. That man was later killed by Jewish partisans. He had murdered seven or eight Jewish children. He would get a price for it—for every Jew, a pound of sugar.

I wandered to the end of the war. I came back to the ghetto and nothing remained—only burned black logs. I met a fellow who survived by jumping off a truck as they were being taken to the graves for execution. He told me my mother, brother and sister were on that truck. My sister jumped off also, but she was shot and then run over for fun. She laid there in the snow all winter.

*   *   *

I survived alone of my family, alone out of my friends, alone out of almost the whole community. Why did I survive out of so many people? Why did I survive? It is really beyond all comprehension. It is unbelievable that I didn't perish—how is it possible? My mother, my father, had more right to survive than me; my sister had more right; my brothers, they had more right. Compared to them, I am simple trash. I am nobody at all.

I don't need or want sympathy from anybody. I just try to explain a few experiences that happened in my life. The stories I could tell you are endless, but it would serve no purpose. It is to no avail. It is a hopeless situation, and my little stories won't change anything. They are minor, insignificant. I know people whose suffering has been far greater than my own, so who am I to talk? The fact remains that people have their own problems to contend with. They are busy raising children . . . and I am nothing and nobody. So my stories are all in vain.

I might be considered disturbed because I did not manage to reestablish and resettle myself as did most of the survivors. Many have gotten married and have raised children. They have tried to seek a normal life and normal enjoyments . . . television viewing, and maybe vacations or something. If they have the willpower to live, God bless them, I wish them well; but my mind dwells over there on years past, years gone by.

I could not get adjusted to something new knowing what happened and knowing the attitude of the world. I got out of the war with all kinds of confusion in my mind. I didn't know what happened, what was going on. I neglected my own personal life. At certain crossroads of life, I got lost altogether. I made mistakes about acquiring proper skills, and I had to go through great hardships of employment. I am a failure, but that is okay with me.

I never married. I'm probably going to die a bachelor, but it doesn't matter. I am not so anxious to marry and raise a family. If it is true what the demographers say, the population of the earth will soon double from four to eight billion. The terror and violence will be great when people run out of the means of existence. The time is coming when

people will devour each other, and others will be sitting
at their televisions and watching it.

*   *   *

I am an exhausted man. It takes all my energy just to
pay the rent and the bills—just plain survival. Life to me is
a horror, a struggle from beginning to end. So I manage to
survive, but I am nothing and nobody. I am totally insignificant. I have no children to support, no old parents to
support. For me, life is senseless and has no meaning. They
used to say in the ghetto that there will come a time when
the living will envy the dead.

I am at the end of the line, so to speak. I have no sympathy for myself of any kind. It doesn't worry me, it doesn't
matter to me. It doesn't matter to me at all. When I was
young, the imagination wanders to faraway places. The
girls, they look so beautiful, and marriage is so important.
The young mind makes it look as if everything is so attain-
able. The fantasies are strong in spite of all the troubles.
The dreams for the future are overwhelming. At this age
it is no longer so. One must always think about the end
around the corner. In my own little mind I know the end
has come.

I would not mind to die. I would be very happy to do
it. Not because I'm angry, but I have run out of energy
and have run out of interest. I don't want to wait for old
age and helplessness. Why should I wait. So one might ask
me, how come I'm not doing anything about it. I don't
want to use a gun against my head. Hanging? No, that does
not appeal to me. You see, I want to make sure it is successful. I don't want to be taken to the hospital and go
through monkey business. If I had an easy way out, I would
do it within a week. I would leave a small note where to
bury me and that would be it. Very simple. No monkey
business and no tragedies. I know I sound like an idiot, but

I would pay to anybody up to two thousand dollars if I could get cyanide potassium. Then I wouldn't sound as if I talk about it and I don't do it.

It might be done. I don't know when. Chances are, the time is nearing. The decision might be made, and if a decision is made, no trouble, and no anxiety. A clean house and a small will, a few shots of apricot brandy and fifty pills, and everything is set. They speak about the survival of the fittest. But even to the fittest of survivors there comes an end.

8

Growing Old: Death in Life

WHAT I EXPECTED

What I expected, was
Thunder, fighting,
Long struggles with men
And climbing.
After continual straining
I should grow strong;
Then the rocks would shake,
And I rest long.

What I had not foreseen
Was the gradual day
Weakening the will
Leaking the brightness away,
The lack of good to touch,
The fading of body and soul
—smoke before wind,
Corrupt, unsubstantial.

The wearing of Time,
And the watching of cripples pass
With limbs shaped like questions
In their odd twist,
The pulverous grief

Melting the bones with pity,
The sick falling from earth—
These, I could not foresee.

Expecting always
Some brightness to hold in trust,
Some final innocence
Exempt from dust,
That, hanging solid,
Would dangle through all,
Like the created poem,
Or faceted crystal.
                                        —Stephen Spender

The Golden Years

Louise Rolfe, sixty-one, and John Rolfe, sixty-seven, have been married forty-two years. She was a legal secretary; he a sales engineer. Recently they moved to a retirement community in Arizona.

Look at life: the insolence and idleness of the strong, the ignorance and brutishness of the weak, horrible poverty everywhere, overcrowding, degeneration, drunkenness, hypocrisy, lying—Yet in all the houses and on the streets there is peace and quiet; of the fifty thousand people who live in our town there is not one who would cry out, who would vent his indignation aloud. We see the people who go to market, eat by day, sleep by night, who babble nonsense, marry, grow old, good-naturedly drag their dead to the cemetery, but we do not see or hear those who suffer, and what is terrible in life goes on somewhere behind the scenes. Everything is peaceful and quiet and only mute statistics protest.

—Anton Chekhov

LOUISE: If any two people were certain that the decision to give up their jobs and move to a retirement community was the right thing to do, it was us; and yet now, even though we have everything we thought we wanted, we miss our old way of life in so many ways that it is pathetic. We are overwhelmed with loneliness, regret and a longing for what we have left behind. Our hearts yearn for the familiar life, and it is hard to realize that we no longer have a life to go back to.

227

In a sense, we are going through a grieving process: grieving for our family, our friends, our familiar turf, our daily routines; grieving for our sense of worth—if only in terms of the dollars and cents of a regular paycheck, the pressures of getting through each day which permitted us, without realizing it, to keep from seriously thinking about what we wanted to be when we grew up.

JOHN: There were many reasons why we decided to retire. I had run into a new management situation at work; the emphasis was on youth. I felt I had a heck of a lot to contribute, but in the last year and a half or so, I wasn't asked to contribute. Nobody is interested in you anymore. I was literally wasting away.

LOUISE: I worked under great stress getting my job done. I felt physically worn out handling both my job and the housework—I needed a rest. We needed to get away from the stresses and strains of work. We had this idea that maybe we could start a new life.

JOHN: We had vacationed in the Southwest for a good number of years, and we were very fond of the area. We visited Sun City, and we were impressed by the cleanliness of the place. We were never home owners, and all of a sudden here was a home we could afford. We did have some brief misgivings; we wondered what it would be like living with a group of older people, but we just dismissed the thought.

LOUISE: We stayed for a week at Sun City on an offer that they had: You can stay in an apartment and take part in all the recreational activities. They don't bother you at all, so it's just like living there. It was so clean and orderly. . . .

JOHN: It was incredibly clean . . . just absolutely spotless and incredibly beautiful. They had everything there, plenty of shopping centers so you didn't have to leave the community.

LOUISE: It was so ideal that it raised the hair on the back of your head. I said to John that I didn't know if I would like to be around all these old people, but we thought it was just a matter of adjustment. You had to look on the other side. There was no dirt, no broken bottles, no cigarette butts floating in the pool, no young kids horsing around in front of you. It was so peaceful.

JOHN: To an extent we were trying to escape the crime of the city, the dirt, the snow; but we find now that we had escaped from a lot of things we didn't want to: the mixture of a normal society, being faced with all age levels, being faced occasionally with the threat of crime—you wouldn't think you'd miss anything like that, but you miss it, it is part of reality. In a sense, our move here represented a flight from reality.

LOUISE: This is not real life. I used to long for this peace and tranquillity, but the narrowness of this existence casts a shadow over your contentment. I read long ago of an experiment where volunteer subjects were immersed in a tank of water. Their eyes and ears were sealed and they were deprived of all sensation. In a short time, they couldn't bear it. Crazy, isn't it, but you kind of get that feeling here that you are in one of those water tanks: no litter, no blacks, no crime, no yelling kids, no noisy cars, no pollution, no rain, snow, cold. . . .

JOHN: It's unreal, the sterile atmosphere; the antiseptic feeling you get is all-pervasive. The shutting out of what's happening in the real world. I am amazed at how few people here read the *Arizona Republic*; yet on the other hand, about ten times as many people read the local newspaper.

LOUISE: The daily Sun City newspaper treats the world news with about four or five lines; Arizona news with three lines; and the Phoenix news with two. The rest of the paper is filled with who won yesterday's tennis match, who made holes-in-one and what kind of iron he used doing it, stuff like that. The whole paper is filled with junk.

JOHN: By and large it is almost as if the people here are reverting to childhood. I think this is a reflection of the unspoken fear of the approaching end. By reverting to childlike attitudes and values, they don't have to face it.

LOUISE: I wrote a letter to someone, and on the return address I put S.C. (second childhood), instead of Sun City. It just popped into my mind that the initials stand for both. There definitely is a second childhood atmosphere here. It's like a Disneyland for senior citizens—*senior citizens,* I've grown to hate that word. There is no want of things to do and clubs to join. We've got a whole sheet of activities that we can engage in, from lawn bowling to bridge for non-smokers.

JOHN: The zeal with which they approach these recreational activities—it's not just playing golf once a week, it's every single day or twice a day.
Even the churches here take on the antiseptic and childlike character of the community. The moral atmosphere is completely sterile. Nobody discusses moral values or issues, whether they concern society as a whole or, more importantly from a Christian standpoint, you as an individual.

LOUISE: It appears to be a major characteristic of every

church you go into, no matter what denomination, that no real basic issues are ever faced. Everybody is so up and cheerful. It's like you don't belong here if you're going to be "negative" and "gloomy." To me, this isn't reality.

JOHN: Churches around here resemble Rotary Club meetings. What goes on is what I call hummingbird religion: Don't get anybody upset by talking about real issues such as loneliness and death. What you get is, "Are you discouraged? Do you feel some days like you'll never get that old golf ball in the cup? . . ."

LOUISE: Everything is sunshine and flowers. I can't believe that people really feel that way. They seem to have an "I'll smile for the world" philosophy: Well, if I'm blue, I'm not going to be showing it to anybody. There is probably a sizeable number of people here who feel as we do that this is a living death, but those people are hard to find.

JOHN: If you scratch the surface, occasionally you get a glimpse of it. Liquor is available everywhere. No matter what kind of store you go into, they sell booze. I've become aware of how often the shopping carts you see don't have quarts in them but half-gallons.

Since we've been here, we haven't had a single neighbor tell us anything they really don't like about this place. Everything here is sweetness and light, and there is absolutely no criticism of any kind.

LOUISE: We were naïve in the beginning. We were invited to neighbors' get-togethers. The standard questions were, "Where do you come from" and "How do you like it here." If you said, "I'm not sure yet," they were on guard. If you said, "I'm not sure that we fit in here," they were afraid—you're a square peg and you're pounded into a round hole. The standard answer they gave you was, "Well, if you're going to shut yourself off, you're never going to adjust. You really have to get yourself out and do things." Anytime you express a discontent with life here, the first thing that's said to you is, "Why don't you join a club."

You can join a club and sit there for an hour and come away with a skill or a new interest, but no real personal relationships develop. You can't have a heart-to-heart talk with anybody.

JOHN: Nobody will entertain a serious discussion. The conversations we have with people around here, no matter how we attempt to steer them, remain on a superficial level. All our neighbors are very nice, but after you've heard the same things repeated five or six times, your tendency is to shun them after a while.

LOUISE: Maybe it's the old folks' way of life. People seem to be willing to spend unlimited hours telling and retelling every little thing about their lives. We live in mortal fear that if we stop hating it here and try to accommodate ourselves, this will become our way of life.

We say to each other that maybe in a year we'll feel better. After a year, don't you even get used to being in prison? Maybe by that time we will have lost some of the anguish of losing our contact with family and friends; but by that time we will have surrendered something within ourselves that is vital. We look at each other and say, do we want to be without that feeling of anguish and pain. When I lose the pain, I will have lost a part of me. If I forget my family and my friends, if I forget the use that I was at my job, I will be a lesser person for having forgotten it. I will no longer be a full human being.

John and I have shared a feeling of not being afraid to die. The fear of death exists for us only in not wanting to be left behind when the other one goes. I find now that I have a kind of wariness of death. Since we're here, I have a kind of sadness. I can't unravel it yet, but it has something to do with . . . is this the way I want it to end.

I don't feel that this is the place where I can be doing those things that I want to be doing. I truly want to be thinking and caring and communicating with people. John is always saying something about not going gently into that good night. I think he means: I want to die struggling, pushing against something, fighting with something.

There is a line, kind of corny maybe, that I cut out of the paper a while ago. It started with, "Let me die laughing, let me die working, let me die thinking." . . . I don't want to die here.

A Change of Scenery

Winnie Fairchild, ninety, lives alone, maintaining her independence despite the limitations imposed by her age.

It's no fun sitting around being a burden to people. You are cut down to size, and your size is about that big. I have to analyze each situation and encounter that I have with my "loving," well-meaning, well-intentioned friends and say to myself, is this impulse out of pride or is it self-reliance.

I believe in self-reliance, but if you are going to worry everybody to death by being self-reliant, then it's questionable. This question of being a burden to people is a terrible thing to carry around with you, just horrid.

I'm getting a little sick of all this.

I think death is kind of fun. I can't wait; I'm looking forward to a change, you know.

Hanging On

Jesús Ortega, eighty-one, lives alone in a room in a boarding house.

I'm telling you
There's no use
in hanging on
You feel like one of those men
without a home or a country
A refugee
I have no family
Mother, father gone
Brothers are gone
Who will take care of me?
I don't like to think of tomorrow
What is there tomorrow?

The Sinner

Katherine LeBlanc, ninety-two, is a resident in a home for the aged.

All these people here
Are waiting to die.
They are old,
And have lost their homes.
Just thinking of death all the time.
When you die—
Only then do you begin life.
There is no one in this world
Who has not sinned.
Not one.
That is what we are suffering for.

Waiting It Out

Viola Johnson, eighty-six, is a resident of a county nursing home.

Life is not lost by dying! Life is lost
minute by minute, day by dragging day,
in all the thousand, small uncaring ways.

—Stephen Vincent Benet

Now that you are old and you need help, you feel, why do I have to suffer?

You don't know what it's like in these institutions. If only someone would come and do some little work—make something, or have little gatherings together and talk. All you have to talk about is what's going on here—you don't know the outside world. If someone could only take you out for a ride or to their home for dinner—anything like that, just to get away from here for a day.

I just walk around here the same as the other people. I get my sleep at night and do the same the next day. I just have to wait 'til my number is up; just hope I'm taken out of this pretty soon.

I look forward to going out.

A Matter of Convenience

Judith Busse, seventy-six, has been in a home for elderly women for less than two weeks.

The younger people are not too eager to have older people around. I was living with my son and his wife and they decided that they would like to live alone—just the two of them. He said to me, "Mother, I know that you are not too happy here, you would live longer and so would we. . . ."

I was shocked. I was really shocked. You see, I had been brought up in a big family—my mother had nine children and we were very, very close. I didn't know what to do.

He spoke to a woman who was a social worker. She had these places where old people could *conveniently be put.* He told me that he found a place which they recommended and it was a clean place . . . so, I got my things together and came here.

This is the first time that I have been away from my family, from my home.

I am a loner now.

A Small Request

Susan Koenig, eighty-eight, is a resident of a private nursing home. Her family has not visited her in more than a year.

We live too long. Yes we do. I'm not talking about people who have their health and have money—they are able to have their own home and can live wherever they want to live. They don't have to depend on their children or anybody else. Then I would say, fine, live to a hundred or a hundred and fifty for all I care. I personally do not want to live any longer.

There are so many things that go wrong with you when you get older. Believe me, each year it gets worse. It's not easy, and you can't do anything about it. Why should you want to stay here and go through all this day after day for no good reason.

I've lived enough, that's the way I feel about it. What good am I? Nobody needs me, so what reason is there for my existence. There is not one reason in the world why I should stay here. I'm no good to anybody, not even to myself . . . yet I have to stay because I can't find anybody who will give me a pill.

I'm not depressed; I can laugh at myself which some people can't do. I think I got a pretty good sense of humor; that's probably what carries me through. I'm not frightened, I just wish I could go and get it over with. What I really would like to do is go to sleep.

239

Rocking Chair Gus

Gus Anderson, ninety-one, has outlived his wife and children. He has spent the past nine years in a rest home.

> . . . *And some men eased themselves like setting hens into the nest of death.*
>
> —John Steinbeck

I haven't got much goin', I'm a dead issue
The only thing I can do is
smoke
      smoke
           smoke
Outside of that I'm "Rocking Chair Gus"
Just sit around
Look things over
      Look at televisions
           Look at the old airplanes
They're the only things we got here to look at
(the only thing I'm capable of)
If I go tomorrow
All right
I go
Ready any time
Anyhow, I take it as it comes
don't care
this way or
that way

Any time He says: Psssst C'mon
I'm ready and happy
Just lay down, close my eyes, stop breathing
disappear
and that's the end of me.

Epilogue

But for This . . .

Written by Lajos Zilahy. Translated by John Parker.

He didn't stop to wash the turpentine from his hands, but merely dried them on the rag that was hanging on a nail behind the door.

Then he untied the green carpenter's apron from his waist and shook the shavings from his trousers.

He put on his hat and, before going out the door, turned to the old carpenter who was standing with his back to him, stirring the glue. His voice was weary as he said,

"Goodnight."

A strange mysterious feeling had shivered in him since morning.

There had been a bad taste in his mouth.

For a moment his hand would stop moving the plane, and his eyes would close, tired.

He went home and listlessly ate his supper.

He lived at an old woman's, the widow of Ferenz Borka, in a bare little room which had once been a woodshed.

That night—on the fourth day of October, 1874—at a quarter past one in the morning, the journeyman carpenter, John Kovacs, died.

He was a soft-spoken, sallow-faced man, with sagging shoulders and a rusty mustache.

He died at the age of thirty-five.

Two days later, they buried him.

He left no wife, nor child behind, no one but a cook living in Budapest in the service of a bank president, by the name of Torday.

She was John Kovacs' cousin.

Five years later, the old carpenter in whose shop he had worked, died, and nine years later death took the old woman in whose shed he had lived.

Fourteen years later, Torday's cook, John Kovacs' cousin, died.

Twenty-one months later—in the month of March of 1895—in a pub at the end of Kerepesuit, cabbies sat around a red-clothed table drinking wine.

It was late in the night, it must have been three o'clock. They sprawled with their elbows on the table, shaking with raucous laughter.

Clouds of thick smoke from vile cigars curled around them. They recalled the days of their military service.

One of them, a big, ruddy-faced, double-chinned coachman whom they called Fritz, was saying:

"Once my friend, the corporal, made a recruit stick his head into the stove . . ."

And at this point he was seized by a violent fit of laughter as he banged the table with the palm of his hand.

"Jeez!" he roared.

The veins swelled on his neck and temples and for many minutes he choked, twitched and shook with convulsive laughter.

When he finally calmed down he continued, interrupting himself with repeated guffaws.

"He made him stick his head into the stove and in there he made him shout one hundred times 'Herr Zugsführer, ich melde gehorsammst'* . . . poor chump, there he was on all fours and we paddled his behind till the skin almost split on our fingers."

Again he stopped to get over another laughing spell.

* 'Sergeant, I report most dutifully'

Then he turned to one of the men. "Do you remember, Franzi?"

Franzi nodded.

The big fellow put his hand to his forehead.

"Now . . . what was the fellow's name . . ."

Franzi thought for a moment and then said: "Ah . . . a . . . Kovacs . . . John Kovacs."

That was the last time ever a human voice spoke the name of John Kovacs.

On November the tenth, in 1899, a woman suffering from heart disease was carried from an O Buda tobacco factory to St. John's Hospital. She must have been about forty-five years old.

They put her on the first floor in ward number 3.

She lay there on the bed, quiet and terrified: she knew she was going to die.

It was dark in the ward, the rest of the patients were already asleep; only a wick sputtered in a small blue oil lamp.

Her eyes staring wide into the dim light, the woman reflected upon her life.

She remembered a summer night in the country, and a gentle-eyed young man, with whom—their fingers linked— she was roaming over the heavy-scented fields and through whom that night she became a woman.

That young man was John Kovacs and his face, his voice, the glance of his eyes had now returned for the last time.

But this time his name was not spoken, only in the mind of this dying woman did he silently appear for a few moments. The following year a fire destroyed the Calvinist rectory and its dusty records that contained the particulars of the birth and death of John Kovacs.

In January, 1901, the winter was hard.

Toward evening in the dark a man dressed in rags climbed furtively over the ditch that fenced in the village cemetery.

He stole two wooden crosses to build a fire.

One of the crosses had marked the grave of John Kovacs. Again two decades passed.

In 1920, in Kecskemet, a young lawyer sat at his desk making an inventory of his father's estate.

He opened every drawer and looked carefully through every scrap of paper.

On one was written: "Received 4 Florins, 60 kraciers. The price of two chairs polished respectfully Kovacs John."

The lawyer glanced over the paper, crumpled it in his hand and threw it into the wastepaper basket.

The following day the maid took out the basket and emptied its contents in the far end of the courtyard.

Three days later it rained.

The crumpled paper soaked through and only this much remained on it:

". . . Kova . . . J. . . ."

The rain had washed away the rest; the letter "J" was barely legible.

These last letters were the last lines, the last speck of matter that remained of John Kovacs.

A few weeks later the sky rumbled and the rain poured down as though emptied from buckets.

On that afternon the rain washed away the remaining letters.

The letter "v" resisted longest, because there where the line curves in the "v" John Kovacs had pressed on his pen.

Then the rain washed that away too.

And in that instant—forty-nine years after his death—the life of the journeyman carpenter ceased to exist and forever disappeared from this earth . . . but for this . . .